God's Heartbeat

God's Heartbeat

A Powerful Premise
for Leading a Christian Life

John H. Clark, III

BFG PRESS
FAIRFAX

God's Heartbeat
A Powerful Premise
for Leading a Christian Life

Edited by Delia Clark

Published by BFG Press LLC
For information address:
BFG Press
P.O. Box 252
Oakton, VA 22124
www.BFGPRESS.com

ISBN 978-0-9820307-0-7

Printed in the United States of America

1 2

PHOTO and COVER ART courtesy of BFG PRESS

Books are available in quantity for promotional or premium use.
Send inquiries to info@bfgpress.com. 10% of profits are directed to charity.

This book is not endorsed or supported by the Department of Defense, the Department of the Navy, the Navy Supply Corps, any representative therein of the United States Navy, or any other governmental agency. Information contained in this book is not official and has either been voluntarily provided or has been obtained from publicly available information.

For my Delia

I look upon life as a gift from God;
I did nothing to earn it.

~ Joyce Cary

Table of Contents

Table of Contents

Preface

Taji, Iraq, July 2004. I arrived in the war-torn city amid total chaos in the Navy's theater-assignment process. As a lieutenant commander in the United States Navy, I was directed to report as the Chief Contingency Contracting Officer "somewhere in Iraq."

Considering the intense war fighting that our nation had endured since the initial Gulf War of 1991, you might assume the Navy and its sister services had a smooth-running operation to facilitate personnel transitioning into Iraq. After all, how hard could it be to send a Naval Officer to Iraq?

Apparently, the Navy had not given much thought to the in-theater assignment process. In late June 2004, while on official travel in Athens, Georgia, I received a telephone call from my boss. He told me my name was on a short list of potential "volunteers" to go to Iraq. I asked him when I was likely to depart for Iraq. His response shocked me. "They need you to leave next week," he said.

So, there I was, facing a short-notice directive to risk my life for someone else's principles, someone else's freedom, and someone else's life. Many years before, as a seventeen-year-old boy, I enlisted in the Navy because I was intensely drawn to the thought of visiting Iraq, Indonesia, and many other countries outside the borders of the United States.

However, as a present-day thirty-six-year-old father and husband, my lofty dreams and boyhood visions had long since been replaced by coloring books, princess tales, stuffed animals, bike assemblies, and thoughts of college financing options. Nonetheless, duty called, and I answered with a flight to Baghdad, via Kuwait.

Actually, *we* answered. My family and I made our respective sacrifices during my tour in Iraq. My wife, Delia, learned to manage the Clark household on her own. Our six-month-old daughter, Sophia, learned to scoot around without me. And on the sweltering proving grounds of Iraq, I soon learned that my heartbeat, my life, is not quite my life at all.

When faced with such a vivid portrayal of The Valley of the Shadow of Death, I soon discovered how slight the razor-thin edge of life actually is. Moreover, I began to truly understand that life is but a heartbeat away from death. Indeed, death is but a heartbeat away as you read the words on this page.

Ultimately, while in Iraq, I learned that my heart beats not because of any iota of my own doing. My heart beats not because I *want it* to; my heart beats because *God* wants it to beat. Thus, it is not *my* heart beat. It truly is...

"God's Heartbeat"

What is Right?

~

"What is right?" I want to know;
"What is right?" to me, please show!
You did, they liked… it must be right.
But hide, you tried, and from their sight.
It's right to "they" and only "them."
Puzzle me! This picture's dim.
To you, it's grey, not black nor white.
But you've no say on what is Truly right.
For even evil, in all its might…
Can *not* take wrong
And make it right.
What is right, now I know…
Right is true, and never slight.
It's *never* wrong…
And it shows its light.

~

John Clark
January1986

Introduction

War is Hell.
~ William T. Sherman

The technical term for Naval Personnel assigned to assist in Operation Iraqi Freedom (OIF) is "Individual Augmentee" (IA), primarily because Sailors are selected on a case-by-case (or individual) basis, as opposed to the Army and Marine corps personnel who typically enter the war zone with a specific platoon, brigade, or division.

As an U.S. Navy Individual Augmentee, I received my training and instruction at the Army's Fort Bliss Post, in El Paso, Texas. At the time, the Army seemed ill-prepared for the influx of IA personnel. And, unfortunately, many of the Sailors and Army Reservists received little more than a rudimentary training in firearms and first aid as they prepared for entry into hell on earth... a place for which there is no adequate preparation.

I arrived in El Paso, Texas, on Sunday, July 18, 2004. The thermometer on my rental car reflected a local temperature of 100 degrees Fahrenheit, a perfect transitional location to gear up for the harsh extremes of the Iraqi desert. For the next six days, I was issued everything from a shovel to a pistol to a pup tent. In fact, I received *too much* equipment.

I actually sent a few boxes of uniforms, tools, and other equipment home to my wife. The choice was clear: send the extraneous equipment home; take it to Iraq; or throw it away. I decided to be safe and send it home.

But why didn't I throw it all away? You may be asking why I didn't keep it with me. Well, after sending the extra equipment home to Pennsylvania, I landed in Baghdad with three duffle bags of gear... three very full, very cumbersome, very large, heavy duffle bags. Still, I kept the extra equipment close (at home) so I could be prepared and practical.

"Be prepared for what?" you may ask.

Well, as former Secretary of Defense Donald Rumsfeld said in various news conferences, "...there are... unknown unknowns." There are those things which we cannot possibly envision happening. But, sooner or later, those unimaginable events occur at the most inopportune times. Entering Iraq, I wanted to be prepared for those events... at least as prepared as I could be with only three duffle bags of equipment. Interestingly, as the Chief Contingency Contracting Officer in Taji, Iraq, I only used my uniforms; I did not use any of the remaining gear in the three duffle bags. While performing my duties, I worked in a small steel trailer, and I lived in a converted two-person trailer. Thus, I had no use for the shovel, pup tent, and multitude of other mandatorily issued gear. But, I was prepared!

Actually, I *thought* I was prepared for war!

During the months preceding my arrival in Baghdad, I had seen various briefings detailing the progress in Iraq (or lack thereof). I had spoken to fellow officers who had returned safely from the war-torn area. And I really *believed* I had a pretty good handle on what I should expect.

Nothing (and I mean *no thing*) can prepare you for mortars exploding all around you... all hours of the day and night. Even the mass-marketed OIF stories conveyed through the media could not delve into the smallest details of what it was like to be in the thick of things.

Imagine:

> *The mortars fell in and around the base with a frequency far more than the frequency believed by the media and almost every American. War is not a 9-to-5 occupation. Mortars exploded in and around Taji at 1400 (2PM) and 0200 (2AM)... and at every minute in between.*

> *The enemy had no set time of attack. Sometimes the small bombs exploded one at a time. During other attacks, the mortars fell one after another for as long as an hour or so... often longer.*

After the bombings, there was a blackout period when all outgoing communication mediums were shut down, pending notification of next-of-kin for those American Soldiers, Sailors, or Marines killed by the enemy's attacks.

No phone calls, e-mails, or other communications were allowed until we received confirmation that family members of those killed in action had been notified.

On some blazingly hot, sunny days, despite the barrage of bombs, there would be no injuries, no deaths, and no shut-down in communications.

On most attack-filled days, though, there was an eventual quiet period on the base, a solemn reminder of the risks each of us faced every single minute of every single day.

We were in a state of suspended consequence... never knowing if, when, where, or how our hearts would beat their last and final beat.

Indeed, *nothing* can prepare you for such an existence. But I knew I had to make sense of the environment. Despite my mind's logic screaming the Truth that "none of this" made any sense, I simply *had to* make the environment palatable; I needed to make peace with my "self"; I needed to quiet that part of me that was logically calculating the humongous uptick in the risk and associated likelihood that I would die within the next ten, twenty, or thirty days.

On the other hand, I needed to believe that I would not die. Quite literally, for sanity's sake, war induces you to choose between fearing the possible... or living the probable. Despite the increased risk of dying while in Iraq, my chances for survival were far greater. Interestingly, as much as the risk of dying increases when we live and work in a war zone, in reality, death stalks us wherever we may roam.

Death awaits the unborn child as she struggles to free herself from the warmth of her mother's womb. Likewise, Death holds a faint grasp on the mother's heart as she delivers new life into our waiting world. Undeniably, Death appears to shadow the elderly. But, in general, Death has no favored demographic. Though morbidity rates vary from continent to continent, Death thrives among man, woman, and child; Black, White, Red, Yellow, and Brown... and every shade in between.

Accordingly, as you read this book, you have the same invitation to the afterworld as the American Soldier deployed to Iraq. Quite simply, no man knows the exact time of his death or the coming of the Lord Jesus Christ.

Thus, much like the Soldier and Sailor entering Iraq, we should prepare ourselves in every way possible for the life ahead. In reality, your entire existence is spent preparing for some type of eventuality.

Proper diet and regular exercise prepare your body for the rigors of life. Proper diet gives your immune system the nutrients and fuel it needs to fend off attacks from viruses and bacteria. The immune system is further boosted by regular exercise. In fact, habitual exercise actually changes the physical composition of your body. Through regular exercise, you will literally get stronger, faster, and better. With regular exercise, you will become better prepared to take on the challenges of life.

In general, the successes and failures of today prepare you for the challenges of tomorrow. And in a very similar fashion, you can prepare yourself today for the mental and spiritual battles that you will surely face over the course of your life. Like a steady diet of delicious fruits, tasty vegetables, and lean meat, a steady presence of spiritual mindedness will undoubtedly lead to a healthier you.

But how do we feed our spiritual minds in the same way we feed our bodies the healthy foods it needs (and wants)? How do we sift through all the sugary thoughts, fatty attitudes, and muddy materials that are ultimately bad for our minds?

How do we best prepare ourselves to deal with *life*?

The answer is in the finiteness of it all...

A well-lived Life prepares us for Death. In the following pages, I will clearly detail a very simple yet powerfully successful course on how to ...

Prepare for your final heartbeat.

1: Life and Death; A Personal Story

The life and career of an officer in the United States Navy is rarely boring. Despite the long hours at sea, months away from family, and years traveling from port to port and city to city, the life of a Naval Officer is full of interesting challenges, remarkable people, and fascinating stops along the way. The responsibilities are far-reaching; and the accountability of a Navy Supply Corps Officer (logistics officer) is on par with a chief financial officer at a medium-to-large commercial company.

Within a few months of graduating from the Navy Supply Corps School in Athens, Georgia, I was detailed to the *USS HOLLAND (AS 32),* a large ship assigned to a homeport in Agana, Guam. While on the *HOLLAND*, I was responsible for the management and maintenance of 1,500 pay accounts. During short deployments, I kept as much as a million dollars in my safe. Since the introduction of the automated teller machine (ATM) and electronic debit machines on our nation's war ships, significantly less cash is carried on today's ships.

However, back when cash was king, I was constantly in a state of perpetual consequence when the time came to balance the books or obtain cash from the local bank. U.S. Navy Disbursing Officers were required to balance their books daily. And, considering the sheer number of transactions occurring every day, failing to balance a multi-million-dollar checkbook on a regular basis could overwhelm the most courageous accountant. More importantly, if there had been any loss of funds, I would have been held personally accountable, and I would have been required to personally repay the lost funds. All the money in my safe had been entrusted to me, as an agent of the United States Treasury; if I lost one dollar or fifteen *thousand* dollars, I would have had to pay it back... all of it. There would be no write-off or discharging of the books.

To obtain cash, I would simply type a specific dollar amount onto a U.S. Treasury Check; present the check to the local bank teller; and then return a day or two later to manually count the hundreds of thousands of dollars. Counting the money was tedious but necessary; I wanted to avoid any possibility of a potential loss of accountability of funds. I did not want to risk losing one single dollar.

When my staff and I traveled to and from the bank, we were always protected by a bevy of armed escorts. The Navy Master-at-Arms were there to ensure our safety, and I was always comforted by their presence.

As the custodian of so much cash, I rarely relaxed. In fact, there were some days when I was probably a little paranoid. I'm not sure if it was simple paranoia, or if my sixth sense was trying to tell me something. Sometimes I just had a nagging fear that an armed robbery was imminent. In those instances of fear, I would simply postpone the bank trip until another day.

In retrospect, I wasn't really afraid of being robbed; I had already been subjected to a robbery experience when I delivered pizza for Dominos Pizza back in 1987. The fear that grasped at me while I was on the *HOLLAND* was more related to a *fear of dying*. I surmised that, if someone was brazen enough to rob a Naval Officer during a daytime bank withdrawal, a murder wasn't too far out of the realm of possibilities. Luckily, nothing along those lines ever happened to me.

However, as I look back, I can see that, for me, the concept of death has always been an important part of life. I have always understood that, to truly live, we must first accept the fact that we will surely die. We must embrace the concept of death, and never look at it with any degree of fear. Regardless of the intensity of our daily battles with life; apart from the trials and tribulations we encounter with friends, families, and enemies, death is as much a part of life as is the meals we eat every day. The sooner we realize the veracity of death, the sooner we begin to appreciate the length of a minute, hour, or day. Indeed, once we accept death as an inherent, inseparable part of life, we can begin to truly understand the finiteness of life.

VISITING A FRIEND

I was stationed on the *HOLLAND* for a little over two years, and in 1996, I departed Guam and transferred to Naval Air Station Corpus Christi, Texas. I spent a few days of much-needed leave (vacation) during the transfer and decided to visit my family in Michigan, and then on to see my good friend, Victor, in Raleigh, North Carolina. And, since I had recently purchased a new sports car, I decided to drive from Michigan to Raleigh; and then on to the air station in South Texas.

As I exited Interstate 85 in Raleigh at three o'clock in the morning, I was eager with anticipation, mostly because I had not seen Victor since I left the United States to live in the South Pacific (two years earlier). Victor and I had kept in contact via letters and trans-oceanic phone calls; but I was looking forward to just hanging out with him; I knew a face-to-face visit would be far better than reading his long, entertaining letters. I was sure of this.

As I drove the sports car into the driveway on Mason Drive, Victor met me in the front yard, smiling and lavishing praise on my shiny new car. But my car wasn't the only thing different. Victor had gotten his ear pierced. Actually, both ears were pierced. Well, more specifically, he had three holes in each ear, a nose ring, and a "dumbbell" punched through his left eyebrow.

Now Victor is a large, boomingly gregarious man with the personality of the world's number one party host. Immeasurably dynamic and witty, he had been somewhat of a cornerstone in my own dynamic life. Nine months older than I and sporting a shaved head, Vic and I had shared great times while we were earning undergraduate degrees at Memphis State University. Accordingly, Victor was actually closer to me than my two brothers living in Michigan. As the early morning stretched into dawn, Vic and I discussed everything from acupuncture to Zionist activities, and from monogamy to monotony.

We discussed in detail the specifics of his wife's recent departure; she had left three days before to go live with her mother in Houston, Texas. In most situations, this would be rather traumatic, if not tragic. But, in my opinion, Vic and his wife had been living on different planes since the three of us had lived in Memphis, Tennessee. Sure, they loved each other, but they were worlds apart on the understanding of the principles of what makes the world go 'round.

As the faint grey of the dawn's early light crept across the horizon, Vic and I wrapped up our discussion on the immediate impact of his wife's departure and agreed to defer to the early hours of the morning and get some much-needed rest. But before I hit the sack, Vic delivered the crushing blow I had sensed approaching throughout our early morning conversation:

His father was dying of cancer.

I went to sleep with a heavy heart that morning, reflecting on the magnitude of emotions with which Vic must have been struggling. I pondered on death and what it meant to me as I lay wondering what I could do to fully support my best friend. Up until the situation with Vic and his father, my experiences with death were very limited. In fact, the only relative that I had known to die was my great grandmother.

APPRECIATING MY HISTORY

When I was a curly headed nine-year-old boy, I saw but did not truly experience the effect death can have on a grieving family. My paternal great grandmother had died in the summer of 1978. I still recall feeling guilty because, for reasons beyond my youthful mind, I did not feel or communicate the magnitude of grief that my parents and grandparents expressed in the hospital grieving room. I was there when the nurse and doctors walked in. I heard the apologies, explanations, and the medical jargon. I knew and understood the finality of the situation. And yet I was more stunned at the outpouring of grief by my grandfather than I was at the reality of the permanent loss of my great grandmother. I watched in pained curiosity as my grandfather repeatedly suppressed, then involuntarily released, powerful sobs and moans of deep guttural pain and loss.

After my great grandmother's death, life did not seem to significantly alter course one way or the other. It was not until many later years that I began to realize the significance of her departure from this world. A former resident of Columbus, Georgia, my great grandmother had seen the worst of times, and the best of history's changes. During summer vacation, my brother and I were elated yet incredulous while listening to her as she told us stories of the not-so-distant past.

However, being inquisitive little boys, we were more fascinated by the red Georgia clay, fire ants, and blazingly hot summer days; we didn't see any value in listening to the stories of her days gone past. Little did we know or understand the power of those days or the concurrent weight those days would continue to press upon each passing moment of our country and its socio-political foreground. We spent more time jamming jalapeno peppers down the throats of toads and frogs than contemplating the economic hardships of our forefathers in the land of the free.

In retrospect, I suppose the life of an eight or nine-year-old is best enjoyed digging up fire ants under the hot Georgia sun; or watching lightning bugs from afar while unwinding on the porch during a warm summer's night. However, considering the wonderful opportunity we missed at receiving an extended first-hand account of history, I wish my brother and I would have spent at least an hour or two each day drawing upon the immense reserves of a great woman, a genuine scribe of history.

Not long after her death, I realized that, through her stories, I had acquired a wealth of information and knowledge. Indeed, the groundwork was laid for a perfect transformation to wisdom.

A LIFE AND DEATH EXPERIENCE

Twelve years later, during my sophomore year at Memphis State University, I was heavily invested in a new semester of college. It was January, just before my twenty-second birthday. And although classes had already begun, I felt most compelled to see my paternal grandmother, my father's mother. Her health had severely deteriorated since the doctors had ultimately determined her ailment to be stomach cancer, and not the ulcers they had previously misdiagnosed.

Back at Memphis State University, I was a continuous resident of the Dean's List, and very active on the social scene. I was pretty much a hard-core academic machine, working 50-hour workweeks while studying for eighteen college credit hours. I was pushing the envelope, but faring quite well. I was proud of my accomplishments, and I had every reason to be proud.

But I wanted my family to know my endeavors, my pains, my obstacles, my victories, and why those endeavors were so important.

I wanted *them* to be proud of *me*. But, since I was the first person in my family to attend college, how could they have a realistic appreciation for the rigors of academic life?

I was certainly disappointed when it seemed like my family didn't care about my academic prowess. I was even more disappointed when, during my semi-annual visits home, no one asked me about my academic progress. I wanted to inspire them with my tales of newfound knowledge and personal triumph. I wanted to share my victories and explain that each of them had a right, reason, and to a large extent, a *responsibility* to share in those victories. I wanted to discuss world events and local politics. I wanted to know their interpretations of the socio-economic state of the neighborhood, city, and state. I needed to be a shining example of where we could go; what we could be, see, and do. I needed them much more than they needed me. And they failed miserably at noticing that.

Everyone failed to notice... except for my grandmother. She never missed a day to tell me how proud she was of me. I can still see her beaming smile and warm, caring eyes as she would sit on the edge of her bed or slowly pace the house with her cane or walker.

Time stood beautifully still as I sat with her and felt her genuinely sincere and loving presence. We would sit on her enclosed veranda, slowly swinging on an old questionable-but-sturdy porch swing, talking about everything but nothing.

Old times, good times, bad times... it didn't matter. I often wondered if she enjoyed my presence as much as I did hers.

Of course, her cooking kept me there as well!

Her banana pudding recipe, in my opinion, was worth millions. And those pork chops! How can something so good to the palette be so bad for the body? She would fry them with, oh, I don't know... three or four spices, and a secret, sacred pinch of *Grandma Seasoning*, an ingredient that is only acquired after raising several grandchildren and, perhaps, a great-grandchild or two. Those chops would be waiting in the oven, along with stovetop friends like mashed potatoes, black-eyed peas, cabbage, and peach cobbler... oh my!

Speaking of peach cobbler, she was a master of all things sweet! You name it; we had it, in multitudes: upside-down-pineapple cake; German-chocolate cake; coconut-pineapple, lemon, and pound cakes; lemon-meringue and sweet-potato pies; apple, peach, and pear cobblers. Trust me; I could fill this page with descriptions of the food with which we were blessed.

And when I returned home that cold January day, I could almost taste the rolls that I knew were rising in the oven. When I saw my grandmother, though, I was devastated by her emaciated appearance.

She was incredibly frail, unbelievably weak, and combating tremendous bouts of pain. As our eyes met, my empathetic senses nearly paralyzed me with pain and a powerful sense of loss.

At least seventy-five pounds lighter than the previous time I had seen her, she greeted me with her best smile and managed a snug hug around my 5'11", 170-pound frame. We talked a bit about school, the family, and "*stuff*." But we knew nothing mattered; nothing mattered in the sense that only our presence there together mattered... nothing else mattered.

My grandmother died the very next day.

My anger simmered up from beneath the surface of my soul. I was angry at God for not explaining life and death; I was angry at my school and my job for not allowing me to spend more time with my grandmother. I wanted to lash out at anyone, everyone. "*It wasn't fair!*" I thought. She was far too important to leave. There were many, many things left unsaid and incomplete. I was most angry, though, with myself. I had not taken the time to fully appreciate and make the most of those final minutes with my grandmother; I should have been there to say goodbye. I needed closure, and I wasn't going to get it. And it was my own fault. I felt ashamed, alone, and apologetic. Most devastating, though, was the family void that was to follow. It scared me more than my own death. For without her, I knew the death of our family structure was not far behind. And that familial death would be the equivalent of a slow, agonizing death... bitter, painful, and even warlike in nature. She was the Queen of our family. And now our Queen was gone.

2: Life and Death; One Life or Two?

What exactly is death? What is it about this fantastic ending that so fascinates and yet terrifies the least and most of humankind? None of the living has experienced it, at least not to the extent where others can be absolutely certain of its characteristics. Sure, we've all heard tales of reincarnation or "walking into the light." But how many of us are willing to literally stake our lives on such tales or dedicate every waking moment to the belief (or non-belief) in an afterworld?

Who among us has such profound beliefs in the *hereafter* that "the *here and now*" becomes secondary? What daily or hourly preparations and salutations have the "true believers" initiated that best exemplifies a fanatical dedication to the simple concept of life... or death.

The two concepts of life and death are actually painfully simple. However, people have a tendency to complicate the obvious. Life and death are the two certain common aspects each of us will face.

Yet we concentrate most of our humanistic efforts at prolonging the time between the two, instead of understanding how to enjoy both, if that is indeed possible. I must emphasize the last contingent point of the previous sentence: *if that is indeed possible.*

For is it really possible to enjoy this life without jeopardizing enjoyment of the next? The answer to this question is prefaced by yet another question, specifically: Is there (another) life after death? More to the point: Do you absolutely, truly, and positively (**without a doubt**) believe in life after death? The distinction is there to relate the fact that a mere passing belief in the existence of life after death will not necessarily dictate or encourage you to change your behavior.

For example, I know driving a car excessively fast can dramatically increase the risk of an accident and a commensurately catastrophic death. Notwithstanding this knowledge and belief, I have, at times, sped well above the posted speed limits. Despite governmental and industry warnings, millions of people destroy their bodies with powerfully poisonous sticks of toxic tobacco.

But you, my friend, are blessed with the power to choose. You can choose anything and everything that specifically concerns your associated actions. And what a fantastic power it is (to be able to choose)!

You can actually *choose* to believe in life after death. But your choice to believe in life after death is pointless if you fail to make the correct decisions on matters related to moral and ethical standards of living.

In other words, if you truly do believe in life after death, are you actually living a life dedicated to that belief?

Let's not get ahead of ourselves. The greatest question remains: does another life follow the death of your current life? If your answer is a resounding, "No," I am confident the later chapters of this book will soften your stance a bit. If your answer is "Yes"; if, indeed, you *think* you really do believe in life after death, I am compelled to ask you: Are you fully prepared to defend that belief? Are you prepared to *die* for that belief?

Please understand the simplicity of these questions. Also, please understand the simplistic beauty reflected by your answer to these questions. If you believe in life after death, you have placed a greater value on both of your lives than, say, someone who does not believe in the hereafter. The two lives to which I am referring include your current physical life on earth; along with a second life, the life lived in the hereafter. If there is a cause-and-effect relationship between your current life and the life lived hereafter, the quality of your life hereafter will (probably) be determined by your actions completed during your current life here and now.

Follow this train of thought: if you believe in life after death, you believe in the existence of the human spirit (a separate, unseen entity).

If you believe in the existence of the human spirit, then you probably believe in God. If you *truly* believe in God, you will follow His teachings. If you chose not to follow God's teachings, you will suffer the wrath of God.

If and when you suffer the wrath of God, you will probably wish you had chosen a vastly different lifestyle than the one you led here on earth... which brings us back to the power of choice.

How are you choosing to live your current life? Of course, it is *your* life. Thus, it is *your* choice to live *your* life in any way *you* choose. No one can make you do anything. When it comes to making us do what we do not want to do, other people are actually powerless.

In fact, contrary to what immature adults and spoiled children think, our own personal happiness is not determined by the successful act of getting what we want. We are not happiest when we get what we want, but rather when we do not get what we don't want.

When we get what we want, our lives may also be filled with unhappiness (and those things which we least desire). Consider the political popularity of the Kennedy family and the fame with which they have been blessed. Many people think they want what the Kennedys have. After careful reconsideration, most people would probably prefer not to endure the significant emotional hardships and painful history of the Kennedys.

On the other hand, some people seem to be happy right where they are, regardless of where they stand on the socio-economic ladder. For these blessed few, their daily joy is cultivated by the *absence* of the things they do not want. We've all heard the admonishment to "count your blessings." The unstated corollary is, "If it doesn't kill you, it will make you stronger." Interestingly, lack of want is not complacency; nor is it a sure sign of success.

However, absence of "don't-wants" is a first indicator of the edges of joy. Notice the distinction between joy and happiness. When one discovers true joy, life itself takes on a certain momentum. In fact, joy is not impeded by death, but actually *reaffirmed* by it, but only if you live according to God's teachings.

We are certain that death exists... we may not know when each of us will die, but we are sure of its eventuality. If we are equally confident that life is eternal, then we can see that a death (from) this life is actually a (re)birth into another life. Hence the concept of "in death, there is life." And if we truly believe that there is another life possible, but only via the death of our current life, our joy is found in ***knowing*** (not simply hoping) another life exists beyond our current travails. And, as the disciple Paul said, "Death has been swallowed up in victory; Where, O death is your victory? Where, O death is your sting?" (1 Cor. 15:55)

WANTS VS NEEDS

Mere happiness is based on external stimuli. Happiness depends on actions outside of your inner self. These stimuli are usually shallow perceptions of what you or other people *think* are important. Examples include degree of wealth (amount of money), types of shelter (size of house), model of car, and the color of your eyes.

Unfortunately, people tend to use these examples to measure a person's value. Ironically, we often use the same measurements when trying to identify how (we think and perceive) others think and feel about us. However, each of us has our own personal worth, regardless of the tangible markers of wealth or physical beauty. Everyone and their spirit is an entity of significance; we are all loved by God.

Unfortunately, unhappiness is often driven by a (perceived) need for other (specific) people and the perceived need for other people's acceptance of us.

As humans, our most basic needs are food, clothing, and shelter. To survive, grow, and maintain a healthy demeanor, our bodies absolutely require food and water. To survive in the midst of nature's elements, we also need shelter from the rain, sun, snow, etc. Socially speaking, we can also say we "need" clothes and social interaction. But since society doesn't really dictate needs, we really don't need clothes. Yes... we can actually live without clothing and conversation. We can't, however, live without sustenance or protection from the elements.

Similarly, you cannot (or, more accurately, "should not") live without considering the **consequences** *of your lifestyle, or the absolute certainty of your death.*

We are usually free to decide among the choices in our life. The consequences of our choices, however, are rarely clean-cut, linear, if-then statements that allow us to see exactly how our future lives will be affected.

Likewise, the impact of a belief (or non-belief) in life after death is not so clear-cut. Nevertheless, you must accept and embrace the surety of your death before you can fully understand the responsibilities of your current life. After you accept death as a natural progression and necessary part of your life, you can begin to accept a certain finiteness of your breath; you can begin to view the world as "end-**ful**" and not end**less**. And, as you continue to witness the death of others, you can begin to realistically deal with these most painful types of losses.

Getting back to the point about food, clothing, and shelter... if confronted with the loss of those primary needs, you will become literally locked into a struggle for survival. The loss of a job, for example, can cause grave concern about how you will pay for meals and shelter. This is a very real and tangible concern. Your job, then, although not one of the listed primary needs, has a direct impact on obtaining food, clothing, and shelter.

Interestingly, your source and place of employment are of great value in American culture. Unfortunately, the *type* of job you have, or where you work has become absurdly important to some people (an example of *perceptions* driving mere happiness).

Keep in mind, *happiness* is far short of *joy*. This is not an endorsement for complacency or an advisement to keep the simplest, most mundane type of job, but rather a discernment of what constitutes a real, bona fide *need* versus a simple, wishful, sometimes wasteful want.

When we lose access to primary needs, we die.

When we lose access to our secondary needs (*our wants*), we lose face, friends, and fancy things. When people refuse to accept the loss of their respective wants, they often begin to believe their very survival is dependent on superficial possessions; and these simple possessions certainly don't fall into the category of needs. We don't *need* toys.

This point is exemplified by observing a spoiled child's behavior when she is denied certain toys, clothes, or any other treasures of childhood. When denied the satisfaction of obtaining their wants, children often become disappointed, angry, and sometimes hurt. Similarly, many adults become depressed or even violent when their wishes are not fulfilled. For example, until a grieving man understands the Truthful concept that losing a loved one is not the same as losing a primary need, he can become entrenched in a debilitating cycle of denial, disbelief, and disenchantment. Our emotions and shared experiences are intricately interlaced, and soon the denial begins to feed the disenchantment, which in turn amplifies the denial... a vicious loop that can have tragic consequences... all based on a misconceived *need*.

Whenever we are confronted with the loss of a loved one, we feel significant disappointment, anger, and agony, among other extremely powerful emotions. These emotional experiences, though seemingly natural, are actually brought on by an initial confusing of wants and needs. Regardless of the type of tragedy (death, divorce, deviated physical condition, etc), humans have the ability to transcend any type of grief usually associated with loss.

However, people have been known to base their very survival on people, places, and things which fall into the category of *want*. As I previously stated, some people become depressed when they can't have what they want. In fact, depression is a classic defense mechanism that people use to cope with a great loss. Some severely depressed people will actually forego their primary needs when overwhelmed by grief. Brokenhearted boyfriends lose weight as their appetite disappears along with their long, lost girlfriends. Surviving members of the deceased often sleep for days, denying themselves food, water, or even the luxury of a shower. As a later chapter in this book reveals, I found myself imprisoned in a dangerous spiral of depression shortly after my return from Iraq.

Why do people do this? Perhaps our actions stem from a refusal to *accept* the loss; a denial and subsequent inability to recognize death as a very real extension of life, albeit the final extension as we currently know it.

ACCEPTANCE OF DEATH

Of course, life is not always about analysis and Truth. Notwithstanding all that I have written here about needs and wants, we can't simply dismiss the concept of grief or the necessity for a grieving process. Death, representing the ultimate loss, requires a grieving process so powerful, so all-encompassing, that we sometimes end up investigating our very own sense of personal worth.

In fact, we feel obligated to assess our own adaptation of life, and our specific version of the truth as it pertains to us as an individual, and not necessarily how the Greatest Truth should be (and is) applied to everyone.

Much of this obligation is derived from our own sense of mortality. When we witness the finality of death, we are reminded of our own humanity, as well as the finality of a decision in which we play a perfect witness and, ironically, a powerless player. Regardless of our social standing, degree of grief, or perceived pact with God, there is no bringing back the dead.

We must, therefore, view grief as a process, and a progression of ideas, actions, and attitudes. And this grieving process must have an ultimate goal and a subsequent result. The progression of those ideas and actions may include memories and thoughts of what could have been, or even characterizations of the deceased. The progression of attitudes may range from despair and loss, to anger and resentment. Regardless of the specific ideas, actions, and attitudes, the process must end in the ultimate **acceptance** of the death and a sincere desire to live another day, with loss, and without our loved one. Perhaps if we take a step back and truly understand the discrete phases in life, we can better prepare to accept the finality of death, whenever it knocks on our family's door. In either case, we *must* remember: it is (and always was) *God's Heartbeat,* not ours.

3: The Elevator of Life

"Choices are the hinges of destiny."
~ Edwin Markham

 While in Iraq, I saw a society that had been driven by a ruthless dictator. Iraq had also been ripped apart by a war that seemed to subject its people to circumstances worse than the conditions exacted by Saddam Hussein. The economy was broken, as were the hopeful spirits of many of the Iraqis. Making the situation worse, many of the neighboring countries were sending insurgents into Iraq, disrupting the precarious peace agreements that had been negotiated between the coalition forces and local sheiks.

As the Chief Contingency Contracting Officer, my primary responsibility was to "bridge the gap" when the multi-billion-dollar private-company contracts did not cover specific mission requirements. Additionally, when satisfying those requirements, my staff and I endeavored to purchase materials from the neighboring Iraqis. By spending money on Iraqi goods and services, we were promoting the local economy and investing much-needed capital back into the war-torn community. In theory, if the Iraqis were busy conducting commerce, they were less likely to lob mortars into our camp.

After spending some time with my staff, I was elated to learn that the two Marine Corps Staff Sergeants were Contracting Specialists; they knew their job very well, and they enjoyed every aspect of their assignment. Both Marines were in the office by 7 AM, and, aside from going to the dining facility, they rarely left the office until well after 10PM. Every day was pretty much the same. Saturdays were like any and every other day of the week... all work, all day, all night. On Sundays, we relaxed a bit and usually arrived at our respective work areas by 10AM. Despite the appearance of a daily routine, life in Taji, Iraq, was never quite routine.

9-TO-5 AND 5-TO-9

Indeed, one of the most difficult challenges was to acclimate to the sheer lunacy of the unpredictable nature of every minute of every day. Roving patrols risked certain death from the sniper's bullet.

Quick Reaction Forces in quasi-armored vehicles were in constant danger of rolling on or near an Improvised Explosive Device (IED). And those of us who spent a good portion of our time conducting business outside the safer confines of concrete buildings were always subject to falling mortar and shrapnel.

The first few days in country were absolutely nerve-wrecking. I had been at Baghdad International Airport (BIAP) for only a few hours when a mortar attack occurred during the evening hours. Believe it or not, no one had ever told me what to do in case of a mortar attack. I had received absolutely no training or recommended courses of action/reaction regarding incoming bombs.

As the mortar struck the ground, there was a thunderous explosion accompanied by what felt like a small earthquake. In retrospect, it was not the very loud explosion that grabbed my innermost emotions; it was the small earthquake accompanying the explosion that struck a rational fear within my personal core. When the enemy and his weapons exhibited the ability to shake the ground beneath my feet, I felt a need to take quick notice and quicker action.

As the mortar hit, everyone in the huge tent scrambled to don Kevlar helmets and flak jackets; I simply dove to the floor and peeked around when I saw that it was the fashionable thing to do. The scene was maddeningly frightful. There we were: men and women strewn about on the floor, in between various chairs, sofas, and televisions. Some personnel had been in country several months; some of us had been there only a few hours. Yet, there we were… all of us peeking and bobbing our heads above the relative safety of the furniture scattered within the confines of the large tent.

That particular attack at BIAP was only a single-mortar attack. However, during the next several days, I witnessed attacks that included multiple blasts and numerous shelling events. For the next week or so, I slowly came to an erroneous belief that my life had lost all meaning. I began to believe in a certain futility. Because of the constant barrage of death raining from the skies, it seemed as if I was losing my ability to think clearly and rationally.

However, it wasn't so much the earthquake-causing mortars that were causing me to become irrational; it was plain ol' lack of sleep. Remember: war is not a 9-to-5 event. The mortars fell all hours of the day... and night.

And, though the daytime attacks brought on a specific type of uncertainty and fear, the nighttime attacks were exponentially more horrific. Without a doubt, the darkness complemented the probability of death in a manner that seemed appropriate. Back in the States, being awakened by any loud noise can be disruptive to a good night's sleep. In Iraq, being awakened in the middle of the night by the forceful explosion and seismic activity of falling bombs... well, that's quite another story.

And, as my own story unfolded over the course of several days, the mortar attacks continued at night. The long days of work mounted, along with the incredible lack of sleep. And, through it all, my mind struggled immensely, simply trying to make sense of a seemingly senseless environment.

Finally, after being in Iraq for about a week, I arrived at an epiphany: if I did not reconcile the significant difference between the *possibility* of my death, and the *probability* of my death, I simply could not go on with my stated mission. Surely, we will all face death in our mortal lives. However, upon my initial arrival into the war-torn region of Taji, Iraq, I was subconsciously laboring over the likelihood of my *imminent* death. And those thoughts were beginning to take a significant toll on my mental and physical health.

In other words, I needed to simply accept my death if I wanted to truly live. I needed to *make the choice* to live. Despite living and working in a very dangerous environment; despite facing the possibility of being harmed by someone and something totally beyond my control, I needed to make the choice to ponder on those things worthy of wonderment. Simply put: I needed to make the choice to move on.

And, the choice was truly *my* choice to make.

After I made the decision to accept the possibility (and probability) of my death, a strange irony occurred. I immediately began to see life in a fantastically different light. My actions and responsibilities gained a greater sense of clarity. Ironically, by confronting and accepting the probability of my own death, I revalued my life.

Unlike the earlier attitude where I came to the erroneous belief that my life had lost all meaning, I now saw my life as a powerful cog in the Global War on Terror; I had undergone a personal, professional, and spiritual transformation, all because of one simple choice.

THE POWER OF CHOICE

After my arrival back in the United States, I dedicated great expanses of time to reflect upon that critically important choice. Relatively safe again on American soil, I had the luxury to wonder what might have happened if I had not arrived at that transforming epiphany. More importantly, I began to understand the awesome power of personal choice. All too often, people try to abandon their innately owned personal responsibilities of accepting, owning, and leveraging the power of their respective personal choices.

I have seen countless examples where associates, friends, and strangers blame anyone and everything for the resultant effect of a situation which was initially caused entirely by them. Unlike those blameless people, you should see the power of choice as a commanding weapon against all things which work in opposition to your respective goals.

Unfortunately, many people see choices as "forks in the road," like the capital letter 'Y', where Choice A differs *slightly* from Choice B.

On the contrary… choices are more akin to a 'T' in our respective paths… not so much a slightly different route, but rather a totally different path altogether, completely opposite in direction and principle than the other available journey. (See Figure 1)

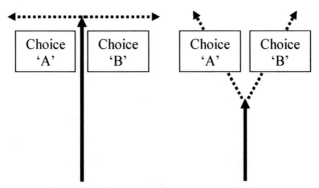

Figure 1: Paths and perceived choices

But how do we recognize and navigate the vast array of choices we face every day? How do we ensure we are making the right decision when selecting from multiple paths, journeys, and routes? How can we maintain an alert mindset to prevent us from erroneously believing our lives have lost a certain degree of meaning?

We certainly can't go around quoting and quipping great philosophers... people would soon grow tired of our presence. And I am certainly not advocating comparing everyday life to the roles, rigors, and responsibilities of a United States Naval Officer deep in the heart of Iraq. On the contrary...

I am asking you to consider the similarities between our lives and the simple mode of transportation called

The Elevator.

In this vast city of souls, our lives are forever flowing into and out of one building and into the next; from one structure to another, in a sea of houses, towers, shops, malls, and associated dwellings. Within these buildings, our lives and minds travel in and out of the various buildings... without a great deal of thought about how we get from Point A to Point B. We arrive at our destination, literally and figuratively, without significant forethought.

We awake in the morning and set a course for some office building, strip mall, or manufacturing facility. In fact, we usually don't spend too much time thinking about how we will get there. But we usually arrive at the correct address; select the appropriate floor of the proper building; and proceed to our office, room, or workstation.

Likewise, in life, the "Elevator of Our Mind" presents us with an excellent opportunity to set the course for our day. And if we can set a daily course of positive thought and action, we can certainly thread seven days together for a week's worth of awesome navigation and choice-making. I'll say it again: if we can start with one beautiful choice, we can (and will) set forth a wonderfully positive day. That wonderfully positive day can actually be partnered with another subsequently successful day, until, before we know it, the week has been a smashing success, and the month is an overwhelming triumph.

Like the physical elevator we see in every tall building, the Elevator of Our Mind starts with one simple choice. As we stand before the closed doors of the yet-to-be-called elevator, we are faced with one sole, simple choice: up or down?

Quite simply,

Which button will you press?

UP OR DOWN?

If you press the "up" button, the elevator will take you up. If you press the "down" button, the elevator will certainly take you down. And in our respective lives, "turning on" a good or bad attitude is as simple as pushing a small button. However, on too many occasions, we blame others for our attitude. We blame coworkers or spouses for *making* us mad. We blame children for *making* us lose our temper. We blame our jobs for *making* us unhappy. We blame, we blame, and we blame. Why do we freely give so much blame to others?

Instead of *giving* the blame to others, we need to accept our respective roles in pressing the single button that raises or lowers the Elevator of Our Minds. We certainly don't blame other people when we get off at the wrong floor of an office building; we don't blame other people if we push the "down" button when we actually want to go up to a higher floor in an office building! Accordingly, we should not *ever* blame other people when our personal attitudes reflect a downward spiral.

Perhaps you think the Elevator of Your Mind analogy is too simplistic; or perhaps you think it doesn't apply to your daily life or how you think. Well, consider what happens once you walk into the elevator in a building. You are faced with another choice: To what floor will you travel? Again, is your yet-to-be-chosen floor above or below your present location?

Likewise, in the Elevator of Your Mind, regardless of how you arrived at your current station in life, you have to make a simple choice: To what location will you go from here? Yes, we all face challenges. Some of those challenges may seem insurmountable. Indeed, some challenges appear hopeless. However, as you stand in your respective box, you are faced with one critical choice: Will your thoughts and actions descend downward into the deep, darkest pit of despair? Or, will you press the "up" button and self-exalt yourself out of the current malaise? It is *your* choice. All you have to do is "press the 'up' button."

Think about it: you can literally travel to any one of the floors in any of the buildings in any of the cities of the world. There are countless structures to enter; and there are many, many floors onto which you can enter. There are floors below you, and there are many levels above your current location. Every single one of those floors is *yours* for the asking.

But you must start by pushing one simple button.

Why is this one simple button so critical? Why do I stress the importance of this ultra-important single switch? I continue to accentuate the importance of this button because it does two very specific things.

First, it puts *you* in control. No one can change your attitude except you. Oh, sure, other people can *influence* your emotions; but, ultimately, the choice to go up or down with your attitude is a personal choice... *your* very own specific, unavoidable decision.

Secondly, this all-important button is actually an elevator "call" button. It *calls* the elevator to your location. Likewise, when you select the "up" button in the Elevator of Your Mind, you actually call a certain amount of positive energy and self-confidence to your self. I know this may sound a bit new-aged or hokey-pokey; but trust me, I'm going somewhere with this. Also, please note the use of the two words "*your* and *self*" as opposed to *yourself*. As you read *God's Heartbeat*, the content of the book will be more easily digested if you see your *self* as something a little bit different than *yourself*.

NO NEGATIVITY!

Think about the last time you traveled in an elevator... Did you notice the "*NO SMOKING*" sign? In the elevator, it really is quite an interesting sign... But, why is this sign in every single elevator?

Of course, in nearly all municipalities, a very specific city ordinance explicitly prohibits smoking while in an elevator. In every elevator, you can find a sign that incorporates a picture of a little cigarette with a circle around it, and a line through the cigarette (the universal sign for "don't do this... or else!"). The words "No Smoking" are presented clearly for everyone to read and heed. (See Figure 2)

Figure 2: Elevator advisory

Why are these signs in elevators? Obviously, as a society, we realize that smoking is clearly a hazard to our health. And as a society, we want to minimize the negative health effects caused by (second-hand) smoking in such a confined space as the common elevator. Let's face it: if you are on an elevator, and someone else in the elevator is smoking... you are also smoking; you are taking in quite a bit of cigarette smoke yourself!

Okay...back to the "No Smoking" sign. That little sign speaks to every single person; no matter who you are; no matter how much money you earn; no matter what your station is in life.

That little sign articulates a simple but relevant message to you and everyone that enters the elevator. That little sign says something about our society: We have chosen to obey the sign that says:

"Hear ye! Hear ye! All who enter the premises of this small space of real estate shall not smoke at anytime as we ascend or descend to various levels of social interaction and physical location."

Indeed, while on an elevator, we have all agreed to make a positive choice *not* to smoke... and to prevent other people from smoking while in the elevator.

Keep in mind... it *is* a choice. There is absolutely nothing in an elevator to physically keep people from smoking. What, exactly then, keeps people from smoking while in an elevator? It is sheer willpower; simple choice; absolute resolve; complete self-control; straightforward self-discipline; unmitigated restraint; overt obedience; subjugated submission; altruistic deference; common respect; ordinary admiration; universal appreciation; and, yes, a certain sense of wonder and awe... We are in awe of a little room called the elevator.

But why are we in awe? What is it about cigarette smoke that keeps us in such a state of awe regarding the relatively tiny space of an elevator? Well, keep in mind that smokers ultimately see the value in rolling down the window in their cars when they smoke. Apparently, smokers like to smoke... but they don't want to share the cigarette smoke with themselves!

Of the people who *do* smoke, they, the smokers, have probably experienced a "time or two" when they have seriously considered a focused attempt to stop smoking. And when they were trying their hardest to quit the filthy habit, they simply did not want to be around (yet) another smoker. Well, I have a proposal for you... and especially you: Why stop at the "No Smoking" sign?

Remember: to choose not to smoke in the elevator, one must have sheer willpower; sheer choice; resolve; self-control; discipline; restraint; obedience; submission; deference; respect; admiration; appreciation; wonder; awe... We are in awe of this little space.

Here's a question: why stop at the "No Smoking" sign? You are now ready to put up a very appropriate sign in the Elevator of Your Mind. Don't stop at the "No Smoking" sign! Your personal sign in the Elevator of Your Mind has your personal circle with a line through it, and it emphatically states: *Negativity is not allowed in this personal space.*

Figure 3: An attitude advisory

Keep in mind: in those physical elevators... all those actual elevators located throughout the city... the signs don't say, "Try Not to Smoke." The signs say, "No Smoking." And, yes, every smoker succeeds at this!

Trust me, I'm going somewhere with this.

ONLY ONE DECISION

Consider this: When you get out of bed in the morning, you are on the ground floor of *your* personal building. It is *your* building. *You* own it; *you* maintain it... and, please understand, *you* make a profound choice as you face the elevator within your personal core. Before you get on your elevator, as you stand there, looking at the elevator doors, you have only one choice.

Please do not complicate this concept. You have only one decision to make as you face your daily elevator. You have only one decision to make today.

Are you going up or down?

The next few days of your life are entirely dependent upon this one decision. If, indeed, you want the attitude of your life to go up... *way* up, please pay attention to every chapter in this book. If you are ready to begin the best, most profound chapter in the book of your current life, please consider accepting and adapting your life to the following analogy (or allegory)...

The Elevator of Your Mind will come when you call it. Your Elevator can go up. And just as easily, Your Elevator can go down. The direction of the Elevator of Your Mind is entirely dependent upon which "button" you press.

You alone choose the direction of your attitude.

You cannot give blame to anyone; you must accept the ability to control and use your thoughts only in the most positive applications.

After entering the Elevator of Your Mind, you will face a multitude of additional choices. There are several floors onto which you can go; some floors are above you; some floors are below you; and you can always come back to the same floor. Regardless of the available choices, the decision is yours. Think about where you want to go in life; then head in that specific direction. You may find immediate success.

Or, you may acquire a vast wealth of unrelated experiences along the way. Regardless of the direct or meandering route of your path, remember: it *is* your path. Accordingly, do not subscribe to the theory of blame. Your path is chosen by you and you alone.

You are who you are. But, then again, you can be who you can be. We all have an inner core of self. For the most part, this sense of self is changeless. Most people would agree that the person they are today is not significantly different than the person they were "a while back." In general, this is a true statement.

However, since we are an aggregate sum of our respective experiences, one particular experience can have a fantastically strong effect on our lives. This effect can be negative or positive. This effect, in and of itself, does not have to be of particular importance to anyone else. In other words: you, and only you, provide the relative importance for that one particular experience.

The previously read chapters of this book are now part of who you are. Please share the wisdom herein. Loan or give this book; speak these truths; and help people change the way they currently think. *You are already a changed person.* You will forever see the "No Smoking" sign and ask, "Why stop there?"

No Negativity, please!

There will be other riders in the Elevator of Your Mind. Some of those riders will want you to smoke while in the Elevator; some will ignore your "No Negativity" sign. Indeed, some people will intentionally ask you to get off on the wrong floor. Don't do it.

Stay focused on being a positive-minded person. Minimizing negativity may seem like a gargantuan challenge in the media-rich culture we currently live. However, in the following chapters, I will introduce a few concepts and tools to help you constructively navigate the challenges presented by negative people, places, and events. The best way to refute negativity is to be positive.

Engage other people. *Share* your positive energy. The more you share your anti-negative sentiment, the greater the confidence you will have to continuously seek and select your chosen direction: using the "up" button.

Sometimes, you will exit the Elevator of Your Mind onto the "wrong floor." Simply turn around, find the Elevator call button, and get back on your specific Elevator. But first, you must choose to go "up." There is always a choice to be made. I choose to repeat this sentence: There is *always* a choice to be made.

If you have had the opportunity to explore the "wrong floor"; learn from the slight detour. If your previous choices seem to have impacted your life in a negative manner, consider what happened; learn from the experience; and move on. This is a choice that *must* be made. Stop mentally laboring over past experiences.

Forget about it! Once you have acquired the lessons from your learning experiences, allow those experiences to float to the back of your mind. The mind has an incredible ability to remember almost everything you have ever experienced (recall is usually the difficult part). Accordingly, don't worry or wonder if you have learned what you were *supposed* to learn.

Forgive yourself; forgive others; and then move on. We have all made mistakes; we have all sinned and fallen short of the glory of God. No one is perfect. And from this point forward, no one will ever *be* perfect. You will make many more mistakes in life; you *know* the person in the mirror will occasionally fumble the ball. Thus, you should not expect *other* people to perform flawlessly in their life. They, too, will make many more mistakes. And you should certainly expect to forgive other people when they *push your buttons.* Moreover, *you are now the only one pushing your Elevator buttons.*

Life, as you will soon see, is painfully simple. We are born, we live, and then we die. In between, each of us has the undeniable ability to create our very own Personal Heaven. We also have the distinct ability to create our very own Personal Hell. In the following chapters, I will present a very simple and direct path to creating and keeping only the Personal Heaven... the place each of us so richly deserves.

If you truly believe God is the owner of your heartbeat, you now understand something called a "Capital 'T' Truth." "Little 't' truths" are mere perceptions and misunderstandings of reality. On the other hand, *Capital 'T' Truths* are indisputable. They can be as general and vague as the color of the sea, yet as specific and True as the crisp morning light of the sunrise as it peeks over the distant horizon. If you don't currently accept the Capital 'T' Truth that your heartbeat is actually *God's Heartbeat,* the following pages of this book will certainly open your eyes to a whole new way of looking at things. *You will see where you once were blind.*

Paul, the Great Apostle, said, "Awake to righteousness." (1 Cor. 15:34) By applying the concepts in *The Elevator of Life,* you can awake to righteousness every day... for the rest of your life. By reading *God's Heartbeat*, you can discover the very real power available to you regardless of what you do or where you work, live, and play. Upon completion of this book, you will understand that your heart already beats for God.

4: A Whole New World

On August 31, 2004, my wife, Delia, and I celebrated our second wedding anniversary. She was in Mechanicsburg, Pennsylvania, and I was in Taji, Iraq. As the Chief Contingency Contacting Officer reviewing contracts and quotes from potential vendors, I had unfettered access to the Internet. Thus, Delia and I were able to send a few love notes and a few pictures of Little Sophia across the miles. Before long, the month of August had slipped into the month of September. Slated for a six-month tour, I was already one-third of the way home.

As a Contracting Officer for the United States Government, I spent most of the workday receiving emails and reviewing the attached bids regarding various reconstruction projects. After my staff posted Requests for Proposal (RFP) on a highly publicized, Government-run website, we would subsequently wait for a multitude of offers from potential vendors to pour in.

The e-mails and proposals were from a variety of people originating from a whole host of different countries. We did business with vendors from all over the world, including Turkey, Britain, the United States, and, yes, Iraq, to name a few.

Most of the e-mails we received were from legitimate businesspeople. However, many of the less-reputable offers were from Iraqi civilians who had figured out how to create and utilize a *Hotmail* or *Yahoo!* account to create a business entity. Accordingly, significant portions of our workday centered on deciphering the legitimacy of the bids we received. Moreover, once we ordered the material and contracted with the vendor, there was no guarantee the troops would, indeed, receive what we had ordered.

Interestingly, some of the proposals were outright funny. Some of the proposals were ridiculously overpriced; while others were incredibly underpriced. Finding the right balance required a continuous review of several factors, including quoted prices, believability of the proposal, proffered quality, method of transportation, and many other small-but-important details. For example, an RFP for a portable light set and generator might garner twenty different responses. One response might quote a price of $15000 per light set; while another proposal would promise to have a set of ten light sets delivered for only $1200. As you can imagine, we spent an inordinate amount of time conducting research, comparing notes, and reviewing historical files.

In general, the sheer diversity of the various proposals kept our jobs interesting. My small staff completed an incredible amount of purchases for the quarter that ended September 2004, and we had begun to see considerable progress on the Forward Operating Base (FOB) that had been recently renamed Camp Cooke. With the fiscal year for the U.S. Government coming to an end, the time had come to send in quarterly and annual spending reports to our headquarters command, which was located thirty kilometers southeast, in Baghdad.

From the introduction of *God's Heartbeat:*
The mortars fell in and around the base
with a frequency far more than the
frequency believed by the media and
almost every American.

I was diligently color-coding an Excel spreadsheet when the first mortar hit the ground a few clicks away. In most cases, we could sense how close or how far away the exploding mortars had landed. Through a combination of Doppler-assisted hearing and seismic sensitivities, we could detect the relative proximity of the bomb (okay... in laymen's terminology: the closer the bombs dropped, the louder the explosion, and the shakier the ground).

On this specific day, the exploding shell was particularly close. As seen in Figure (4) on the next page, my office was a small steel trailer. It tipped violently as I donned my flak jacket and Kevlar helmet while heading out the door toward the nearby concrete bunker.

Figure 4: Contingency Contracting Office, Taji, Iraq
(Notice the bunker in top right corner of picture)

Curiously, the more time I spent in the war zone, the more immune I became to the destructive power of war. After casually walking toward the bunker (which was only about twenty yards away), I suddenly became very aware of the distance between the bunker and me. A second mortar had exploded... significantly closer than the previous explosion. I immediately quickened my pace into a fast trot.

Approximately halfway to the bunker, my left leg twisted and, unbeknownst to me, I ripped the medial meniscus in my left knee. The medial meniscus is the soft tissue that cushions the impact of the bones in the knee.

The pain was immediate and sharp, and, for a split second, given the dynamics of the environment, I wondered loudly in my head if I was experiencing the pain of shrapnel.

However, by the time I had reached the relatively safe confines of the concrete bunker, I realized that I had simply twisted my knee. As the wailing "incoming" alarm sounded overhead, one of the Marine Staff Sergeants asked me if I was okay. Apparently, he had seen me wincing from the pain and clawing at my knee. "I'll be fine," I said.

Ten days later, after a steady diet of painkillers, I was flown to the Air Force Theater Hospital at Balad Air Base. At Balad, I received an in-depth review of my now hugely swollen leg, as well as an x-ray of my injured knee. Soon thereafter, I was flown to Landstuhl Regional Medical Center at Landstuhl, Germany. Interestingly, the Department of Defense policy for returning injured personnel in Iraq was quite firm: If the injury (any injury) could not be repaired within 14 days, the wounded service member was to be medically evacuated (Medivaced) to the United States.

Normally, one would think evacuation from a war zone is a good thing. However, notwithstanding the love I had (and have) for my family, I was duly engaged in an Iraqi mission that was of significant importance to the troops of the Contingency Contracting Office, the staff in Baghdad, and, in a very real way, the men, women, and children of Iraq. This may seem a bit self-aggrandizing. However, let me be clear: by October 2004, I had been in the Middle East for almost three months. I was fully integrated into the coalition functions, contracted-commerce operations, and overall planning discussions for the future of Camp Cooke and central Iraq.

And, though the prospect of seeing my family did shine brightly in the windows of my heart, my inadvertent medical evacuation caused me to unceremoniously abandon my (incomplete) mission. In my own personal thoughts, I had not completed my assigned duties.

Moreover, the self-sustained injury was actually embarrassing. In reality, the injury was a non-combat-but combat-related injury. How does one even *begin* to articulate the specifics of this type of story? Believe me: I fully realize the impending cliché that becomes the introductory phrase *"There I was...* listening to the incoming mortars."

Nonetheless, on October 18, 2004, I exited a C-130 aircraft at Andrews Air Force Base, and was shuttled over to the National Naval Medical Center in Bethesda, Maryland, along with several injured Marine Corps personnel. I was humbled by the Marines' injuries. Some of the men were receiving intravenous fluid. One Marine in particular was in serious condition, beset by medical monitors, IV's, charts, and attendant personnel. He was probably a few heartbeats from facing his Final War. The entire scene was surreal, serene, and simply gut-wrenching. So there I was, in a bittersweet moment of return. There I was, one week removed from bombs exploding in Iraq. Quite literally, I was in a whole new world. And though I did not know it, my entire life had changed; and my entire world was about to change again.

5: The Key to Life

Germany's time zone is six hours ahead of the time zone in the Eastern United States (or eighteen hours behind, depending on how you look at it). Likewise, Baghdad is seven hours ahead (or seventeen hours behind). Thus, when it is noon in Pennsylvania, it is 7PM in Iraq.

In reality...
Everything happens at the same time.

Throughout my continuously changing medical circumstances in Iraq and Germany, I managed to keep my wife and other family members apprised of my situation. Because my injury was non-life-threatening, I had wholeheartedly expected to be given some sort of injections and then be returned to duty in Iraq. So, you can imagine the family's surprise and relief when I called and announced that I would be returning home for immediate surgery to my damaged left knee.

Whenever a loved one spends any amount of time in a war zone, the family wrestles with its own sense of fear and uncertainty. And those fears and uncertainties remain parked at the forefront of their thoughts until the service member physically arrives back at his or her respective home. Ironically, sometimes the anxiety and associated fears increase after the service member departs the war zone. All is not well until mommy, daddy, son, daughter, uncle, or whoever... is safely sitting in his favorite chair, or drinking from her favorite glass.

For Delia and me, a whole new world had begun the very night of my flight from Germany. Despite the simplicity of my injuries... or, rather because of the relatively insignificant nature of my injuries, I would not undergo the required surgery until January 25th, 2005... four full months after sustaining the initial tear to the meniscus while in Iraq.

During the ensuing four months following the injury, the muscles in my leg began to deteriorate significantly. The course of treatment from the doctors at Bethesda was summed up in a few short sentences:

- *You are an active-duty Naval Officer who was injured in Iraq. Bethesda (National Naval Medical Center) gets first right of refusal to do the corrective surgery.*

- *Your injuries are non-life threatening; so we, the doctors, can wait to do the surgery.*

- *Other injured personnel are returning from Iraq with far more serious injuries than yours; thus, since Item #1 and Item #2 (above) apply, you, Lieutenant Commander Clark, will have to wait to have the surgery performed at a date to be determined at a later date and time (TBD).*

- *No... you cannot have the surgery performed by a civilian doctor.*

Figure 5: Aboard a Blackhawk over Iraq

So, there I was... stuck in a medical nightmare, at the very onset of the most intense battles of the Iraq war. The battles in Fallujah, Iraq, were sending scores of injured Marines to Bethesda every week. And in accordance with morals, ethics, and Department of Defense policymakers, my less-than-serious injury was put on hold for yet another day, week, month...

Who was I to question the logic of the attending doctors at Bethesda? Still, I pleaded and pleaded, e-mailed and called, trying to obtain approval to allow treatment by a civilian doctor. All of my actions and pleading proved fruitless.

Keep in mind that my family and I lived in Mechanicsburg, a small quaint community just outside of Harrisburg, Pennsylvania, about two hours north of Bethesda. Yet, I was expected to keep Bethesda as my only choice when seeking medical treatment and procedures attributable to the injury I sustained while supporting Operation Iraqi Freedom.

Before long, I began to consistently push the
"down button"
in my Elevator of Life.

RUNNING ON ANGER

Before my tour in Taji, Iraq, I was an avid runner. I was not a competitive runner; I simply loved the feel of the wind on my ears and the sun on my face. As a passionate writer, I would often meditate on various thoughts and ideas as I ran. Upon returning home from a good six-mile jaunt, I would risk dripping sweat onto the computer keyboard, just so I could capture the thoughts that had recently arrived in my mind during my latest run.

The initial tear in the meniscus was a painful-but-repairable injury. However, after months of limping on the shredded cartilage in my left leg and favoring the strength of my right leg, I was soon diagnosed with Stage III chondromalacia, a deterioration of the cartilage under the knee cap. And for the first time in my life, I was no longer an avid runner; moreover, I was no longer a *capable* runner.

Significant time had elapsed since the initial injury; and my attitude began to shift considerably negative. Indeed, I began to consistently *push the "down button"* in my Elevator of Life. Coupled with the lack of a good physical-therapy regiment, the prognosis and post-operative recovery process following the first surgery were not good. In February 2006, I underwent a second surgical repair to my knee; receiving significantly better aftercare and post-operative therapy.

But those morning and afternoon runs were gone... forever. In retrospect, I should have sought *mental* therapy after both surgeries.

No longer could I escape into the brightest horizons of my mind while sprinting across the neighborhood. Gone were the days of running with my dog, Zeus, along the chosen paths of our daily jogs. Never again could I look forward to running a 5K race or, eventually, a marathon. Never is a very long time. Never is also a very, very heavy word. When the doctor told me that my running days were *over* (his exact word), I winced in psychological agony. I was shocked, chagrined, and, quite literally, in a state of disbelief. I was in denial.

After adding an additional twenty five pounds to my 195-pound frame, I became deeply concerned about my future prospects as a Naval Officer on the fast track. Though I didn't realize it, I began to sink into a soft but powerful state of depression. I was incredulous that my life could go from unbelievable highs to just plain ol' "blah." As discussed in Chapter 2, *Life and Death...*, I was essentially grieving the loss of my ability to run; but I was in serious denial.

At the same time, I felt guilty about returning from Iraq, alive and injured, but injured just enough to be medically excused from completing my mission in Iraq. It seemed as if no one cared, understood, or wanted to hear my side of the story. Ironically, I loathed even casually talking about my plight. I had lost all sense of self-direction.

Adding insult to injury (literally), the Navy detailers were strong-arming me to accept an immediate assignment to a large-deck ship, a requirement that would have wrecked havoc on my not-yet-recovered knee. I tried to reason with naval commanders, captains, and even admirals. But, at every instance, I was told I could not have it both ways... I had to choose between having a healthy career and having a healthy knee.

I was beyond angry. I was incensed.

And when a fellow officer was given a higher ranking than I, despite the fact that he had already been passed over for promotion, I became even more despondent and apathetic toward the Navy. By the spring of 2006, I was a completely different man than the young, brave, bold Naval Officer who had grown personally, professionally, and spiritually while in Iraq. I hated my knee; I despised the Navy; and I secretly harbored resentment against anyone who could run, swim, and play any type of sport requiring agile movements. Flag football was popular on the base, but not for me. There were always pick-up games of basketball at the base gym, but not for me. And I was envious of everyone who could join in on those group-oriented activities.

Though I was spared the bombs and shrapnel in the desert of Iraq, I was now applying a self-destructive train of thought that would eventually lead me to submit a draft letter of resignation and planned retirement to the deputy commander at the base in Mechanicsburg.

I was fully prepared to simply quit.

Then, I purchased a new hybrid bicycle.

Unbeknownst to me, I had stumbled onto another path to yet another Elevator Door. Before long, I would face those same two buttons of destiny. Soon I would gain another opportunity to select from the "up" or "down" buttons in my own Elevator of Life.

CONSCIOUS, CONCERTED EFFORT

My, my, my... what a difference the road makes, literally and figuratively. After little more than a week of riding my newly purchased bike, I began to rediscover a vivid access to my deepest thoughts. And to my sheer amazement, I so thoroughly enjoyed the bike riding; I went back and purchased a bike for my wife... and a small trailer for Little Sophia. In no time at all, Delia and I were making small escapes to quiet places and stopping off for a quick respite with our Bibles.

With each passing day and every pedaled mile, I achieved a new sense of self. This new self was not really comparable to the "Old John." The *Old John* was someone whom I had never really known. He was the guy who was an avid runner... or was he? He was the guy with a strong sense of persistence... or was he? He was the guy who could overcome anything, everything, and anyone... at least until he met the *Real John*. The Real John proved to be my greatest opponent. In reality, the Real John was as much an enemy as were the insurgents in Iraq, but far more insidious and dangerous.

The Real John knew my deepest fears and my greatest dreams. More importantly, the Real John knew how to use those fears to keep my greatest dreams from ever reaching their fulfilled status. However, as I increasingly improved my attitude, I gradually gained the confidence to confront and overtake The Real John.

I disposed of the dangerous dichotomy that existed between the man I wanted to be and the man that I could have been. I made the conscious, concerted effort and follow-on choice to live the day for what it was: a new day in the life of John. I began to see an incredible beauty in the eyes of my wife and child; I heard the birds sing again; I saw the awesome power and splendor of the sunrise, sunset, and every light that shone in between. The Old John was not really back; the *Real John* had actually come alive!

Before long, I began to consistently push the "up button" *in my Elevator of Life.*

ACCEPT, ADAPT, ACHIEVE

And, as I look back on those days of despair, I know exactly what particular, key event spurred the phenomenal change in my attitude, my behavior, and, ultimately, my life. That particular event was actually one specific act among a trilogy of actions that can help you overcome the tallest mountain and the deepest valley.

That one key event was the single act of *acceptance*.

The trilogy of tools that can help you overcome those mountains and valleys are the three specific acts to **Accept, Adapt, Achieve**... in that particular order.

Throughout my entire life, I have always believed the key to life is in one simple action: *The act of Acceptance.* Regardless of the situation, *acceptance* is the key. Regardless of the people with whom you interact, *acceptance* is the key. Despite the magnitude of the consequences you may face at any given time in your life, *acceptance* is the key to solving the greatest or least of your problems.

For, without acceptance, you will continue to live in denial (the opposite of acceptance). Once you have achieved the solo act of acceptance, you can (and will) begin to adapt to those people or events that seem to cause you harm. Once you have accepted and adapted to your given challenges, you *will* succeed and achieve your heart's content.

Make no mistake: **the key to life is acceptance**. You simply cannot change what has already happened. And you simply cannot move to the second key (Adapt) until you first *accept* a few (Capital 'T') Truths about your given situation, regardless of the specific situation.

THE POWER OF DENIAL

A classic study in acceptance (and denial) is reflected in the story of passengers' actions aboard the *RMS Titanic*, a colossal luxury ocean-liner that sank into the frigid waters of the North Atlantic Ocean in 1912.

The ship was afforded the misnomer "unsinkable." Unfortunately, on April 15, 1912, despite being warned that the ship was taking on excessive amounts of water, many of the passengers refused to "accept" the fact that the ship was sinking. According to PBS, it is a well-known fact "that most of the passengers and many in the crew refused to believe she was doomed. In the first-class lounge, the band played upbeat tunes, and for a time there was almost a festive air.

The first lifeboats left the ship far less than full. The one occupied by Sir Cosmo and Lady Duff Gordon, among the Titanic's few titled passengers, rowed off with only 12 on board. Its capacity was 40. Although there were exceptions, the prevailing rule was women and children first. When husbands helped their wives into a boat and waved goodbye, most assumed a speedy reunion."[2]

Since they did not *accept* the reality of the situation, many of the *Titanic*'s passengers did not (could not) adapt to the emergent situation. They did not accept the probability that the ship was sinking; and since they did not adapt to the life-threatening conditions, most passengers failed to achieve a successful escape. *They died because of denial.*

The same can be said for anyone who sits in a smoky room, refusing to accept the likelihood or probability that "where there's smoke, there's usually fire." *Accepting* the prospect of a nearby fire, one can (and should) adapt to the situation and seek an immediate exit. *Adapting* to the situation provides a much higher probability of *achieving* survivability.

There are those who will say that *understanding* is more important than *acceptance*. To them I ask, "Do you understand how your television remote works? Do you understand the electronic interaction between the infrared circuitry on the remote and the receiver on the television? Or, like most people, do you simply 'accept' that, if you push the 'on' button, the television will turn on?" Of course, we all *accept* the function of the remote, regardless of our lack of understanding of its circuitry.

Titanic, smoke, and television... three very diverse topics; each interwoven with the simple concept of acceptance. If you're on a ship in the middle of the ocean, you should probably accept the possibility of sinking. If you are in a smoke-filled building, you should at least consider accepting the possibility of a nearby fire.

You simply cannot change what has already happened.

However...
Accepting and subsequently Adapting to
the situation provides a much higher
probability of Achieving success.

DENIAL

In daily living, the exact same rules apply. *Accept, adapt, achieve.* If your spouse is "causing" you untold grief, accept the reality of the situation. Adapt and make the necessary changes to which you, yourself, can commit; and you **will** achieve your heart's content. Likewise, if you find yourself facing some rather challenging situations, do not turn or run from the circumstances; accept the reality of your position. Please note that "accepting the *reality*" of your situation is not the same as "accepting the *situation.*" If someone is disrespectful to you or harming you in any way, do not tolerate or accept those types of actions. You must, however, accept the given reality... and *then* you can adapt to the situation.

More precisely, accept the veracity of your problems; embrace the challenges you currently face. To do otherwise is a self-destructive form of denial. And you should *never* underestimate the power of denial.

When I returned from Iraq in 2004, I faced an injury that left me unable to run and, in my mind, unable to think. I had chosen to refuse to accept the loss of something exceedingly important in my life. Yielding to denial made me powerless. Accepting my condition, on the other hand, made me powerful. As soon as I accepted my condition, I soared to a possible solution: a new bike. The new bike took me on a literal and figurative path; it brought me face-to-face to a new Elevator Door.

Facing that one large door, I made a momentous decision to push the "up button." From that moment, everything in my life began to change.

You, too, can overcome *anything*. All you have to do is accept your power by refusing to live in denial. Only after shunning my denial did I become powerful. You, too, can be afforded the opportunity to choose the correct path, but only after trouncing your denial and accepting your Truths.

The question is... How can we get to the critical point of acceptance, especially when life, at times, seems so unfair, unreasonable, and just plain ol' unfit to live? The answer: *Accept, Adapt, Achieve.*

ACCEPT

Accept that there is God, the (only) omniscient, omnipotent Deity. Indeed, many people say they believe in God. However, it would be more accurate to say that many people *express* a belief in 'a' God.

If you truly Accept that there is **God** (the omniscient, omnipotent Deity), then you must, by definition, accept the All-Knowing Power of God... which is to say, "I accept His will; **whatever** His will is, it will be." This is what we can term "absolute faith."

Warning: *There is a God. And, yes, there is an anti-God.*

If you accept the *fact* that there is an All-Knowing Powerful God, you should also think about accepting and knowing that there is a very, very powerful opposing force. Though this force is ultimately subject to the All-Knowing Power of the One True God, *you must not underestimate the power of the opposing forces that exist solely to oppose the Power of God... and you.*

ADAPT

Pay attention to the very specific role you play in your life; your own starring role. You are responsible for everything you do. You now own everything that has happened to you. You now own every single thought. You have absolute power to change any/all of your thoughts. Once you have accepted this key concept of life, you are now ready to build on your acceptance.

Adapt to the accepted ideas. If, indeed, you actually accept the ideas above; if you truly accept that there is God; live like there is God, accept that there is evil in this world; and be very, very wary of evil. Accept responsibility for increasing the good in your life; don't blame anyone for anything that happens in your life.

Adapt *now*; the time to change is *now*. Adapt as though your house is on fire, and the only way out is blocked. What will you do to adapt?

Adapt as though you are on the *Titanic*, and there are no more life preservers or lifeboats. What will you do to adapt? Adapt as if your life depends on it. Why?

Your life *does* depend on it.

ACHIEVE

After you have accepted God's will, and after you have adapted to maximizing the good (pushing the "up" button in your elevator), achieving any and every thing is in the possible Hands of God. Re-read the previous sentence. Please ensure you understand this point: anything is possible, including a potential "no" as the answer to your prayers. Jesus himself prayed for a possible release from the Crucifixion, as reported in Matthew 26:42:

He went away again the second time, and prayed, saying,
O my Father, if this cup may not pass away from me,
except I drink it, thy will be done.

And, as witnesses to the greatest event in the history of mankind, we know God was listening to the prayer of Jesus; but we also know God's answer to Jesus.

*Will you truly, absolutely **accept** the belief in God?*

POETRY IN MOTION

Take a moment and refer back to the poem on Page xi of this book. Take a few minutes and ponder on the Truth espoused in the simple rhyme of the poem. Ask yourself if there are any absolutes in this world. Moreover, ask yourself if you absolutely believe in God.

*Will you truly, absolutely **accept** His will?*
...especially when His answers conflict with your wants?

Sometimes God says "No."

There is no grey area; either you believe in God, or you don't believe in God. If you truly believe in God, you will learn to accept the Will of God, which, in reality **is reality**. Once you learn to accept the Will of God, you will begin to adapt to a life that reflects your belief in an All-Powerful God. Once you allow Him to change your life, you will begin to see and understand the great richness that is possible only through Him. Such a newfound sight and clarity of life is an achievement of incomparable value. But remember: Acceptance is the key to life. Do I have your attention yet? *Trust me; I'm going somewhere with this.*

6: May I Have Your Attention Please?

Trust me...
I'm going somewhere with this.

Whoa! Those are such frighteningly powerful words! Perhaps I am asking quite a bit from you. Trust is such an absolute ideal. Trust is such a fragile entity. Trust is such an intimate portrait of a relationship...Or is it?

When I say, "Trust me... I'm going somewhere with this," I am simply stating the obvious. I am only explicitly stating what is merely implied when newspapers print an article; or when media companies distribute Hollywood movies, TV shows, and popular magazines. Every time a government or media official speaks, he or she is asking for your trust. And for the most part, people are very willing to simply give their valuable trust to other people and organizations.

The production crew and anchor person on the six o'clock news says, "Trust me." The day care center where parents park their children says, "Trust us." The large billboard sign advertising food products or financial services says, "Trust me." Everybody, everything, everywhere says... Trust me! The question is: whom *will* you trust? Whom *can* you trust? In whom do *you* trust?

Trust me...
I'm going somewhere with this.

ARE YOU READY FOR CHANGE?

Your brain does an automatic analysis of the information received whenever you read something. When you read a book, you allow the author to take you to a different vantage point; you allow the creator of that manuscript to escort your mind to a predetermined destination. But, to where is the author taking you? You have no idea!

Before I ask you to invest additional trust in this book, please keep in mind that, in many respects, you will be a changed person when you have finished reading *God's Heartbeat*. The world, though not significantly different than when you initially began reading *God's Heartbeat*, will begin to appear different, simply because you will gain insight into a vastly different reality.

Thus, I have a simple question for you: after reading the following chapters, will you continue to live the lifestyle you were previously living? If you actually gain considerable insight in the next few chapters, will your newfound Truth suddenly change your life?

Are you prepared and ready for a step towards a Truth that will allegorically kill off your old self and make way for the new you? Are you absolutely ready to evoke the most powerful winds of change? If you are ready to become the Real You... Trust me, I'm going somewhere with this.

PERCEPTIONS

Remember: For most people, truth is merely a shadow. Most people are not particularly interested in the Capital 'T' Truth; they only want to prolong, project, and protect their own relative *perceptions* of reality. However, Absolute Truth (Capital 'T' Truth) is the *only* reality. If, on the other hand, we believe our own perceptions are reality, then we have summarily dismissed Absolute Truth as the True reality. We have *chosen* to ignore the Truth. We have, in a sense, created a totally separate reality.

Why is this dichotomous concept of perception and reality an important distinction? Well, there are always at least three different perspectives to consider:

1. Your perception;
2. Others' perceptions; and
3. Reality: the way it *really* is.

Interestingly enough, aligning two of the three items requires effort. Aligning all three perspectives often requires gargantuan efforts. But remember: perceptions are merely points of view. Perceptions are viewpoints of reality. Perceptions, by definition, are set in a place that is totally different than reality. Consequently, sometimes… most of the time… perceptions have absolutely *nothing* to do with reality.

For example, my wife is absolutely paranoid about running out of gas in the car. And if the gas gauge reflects less than a quarter tank of gas when I am driving, from *her* perspective in the passenger seat, she is absolutely convinced the vehicle won't make it to the next stop sign. In reality, however, there is enough gas remaining to get us all the way across the city… and back.

From her perspective and thus, her reality, the vehicle is in dire straits. However, *her* reality is not at all related to the certainty, the fact, or the truth of the matter.

As you continue reading the pages of this book, please keep this critical point at the forefront of your mind. It is critically important to realize that we sometimes pay **more** attention to our *unrealistic* perceptions, despite the reality of the particular situation.

By paying too much attention to your perceptions, you are actually ignoring reality. When you ignore reality, you ignore the Capital 'T' Truth.

When you ignore the Capital 'T' Truth, you actually perpetuate your own version of the truth. And, though you may lie to yourself and others, the Truth remains unaffected by your efforts to change it. Reality is Truth Itself, regardless of our ignorance of reality and Truth. In the final analysis, Truth is what **is**; Truth is not necessarily what you **think it is**. Pay attention. *Trust me... I'm going somewhere with this.*

PAY ATTENTION

Take the time to stop and pay attention to what you are paying your attention. Your attention span is a finite resource. Just as your checking account has limited funds, your attention span is limited. And, like the funds paid out of your checking account, your limited attention is "paid" to various people, projects, presentations, and a plethora of other attention-grabbing items.

Periodically, you should stop and take a serious look at the things to which you are literally paying your attention. *Why* are you listening to *what* you are currently listening? *Why* do you watch *what* you are currently watching? Why do you consistently do the things you currently do? And most importantly, how are you affected by those things to which you are paying your attention? How do those seemingly pointless, innocuous messages ultimately affect you, your mind, and your life?

Pay attention to what your five senses are telling you. More importantly, pay extra attention to what you feel and see with your *sixth sense*. Your sixth sense has a tendency to scream at you when you need to be jostled into a new way of thinking or acting. Unfortunately, we have become accustomed to paying all of our attention to external stimuli; we no longer rely on our inner sense of self to help us navigate the realities of this world. We *spend* far too much attention on other people's perceptions; we *spend* much less attention on deciphering the reality of the Truth. And because we are so accustomed to receiving and believing outside stimuli, we learn to suppress our inner sense of self. Ultimately, we deliberately work against our internal strengths while relying on the weak, negative sentiment of a painfully indifferent society. This is just plain wrong!

Pay attention to what you are paying attention.

Consider your television. How much did it cost? How much does owning a television really cost? The purchase *price* of the television's cost is just a fraction of the television's true, total *costs*. You should also consider the monthly subscription costs for cable. Also consider the cost of the electrical power used to operate the television. Then there is the associated power required to engage the VCR, DVD, and game player, not to mention the purchase cost of those items. For the DVD player, you should also include the cost of a video-store subscription, late fees, and expensive video-store candy.

But wait... there are still more costs. Consider the time and transportation cost incurred when you drive to and from the video store (fuel; marginalized vehicle maintenance costs; insurance; etc.). So, again: how much does owning a television really cost?

ARE YOU REALLY PAYING ATTENTION?

When you are watching cable television, does it really matter if the television is physically tuned to channel "three" or channel "six"? The answer to this question, of course, is "yes." Most cable converter (set-top boxes) require the television to be physically tuned to channel three. And there is a significant difference between the programming received when the television is tuned to channel three, and the programming received when the television is tuned to channel six. When the converter box is tuned to channel six, the television will display a screen of fuzzy static and perhaps a few stray signals.

As soon as the converter is changed to channel three, the television world opens up to hundreds of crisp, clear stations. Simply changing the selected channel has a powerful effect on the potential choices of shows. Simply switching from channel six to channel three fundamentally changes the way you watch television! Remember: It is extremely important to pay attention to what you are paying attention.

If the converter is tuned to channel six, the reception will be horrible. Naturally, you will try to improve the reception. Perhaps you will check to ensure the video cables are connected properly. Maybe the incoming cable signal is weak. You could buy more cables. You could call the cable company. Of course, you'll probably be put on hold for an extended length of time. Or, worse yet, you will receive a scheduled appointment "sometime tomorrow between 9 and 5."

If you are doing all this, you are simply not paying attention to the right things. All you really need to do is change the channel from six to three.

But first, you need to pay attention to what you are paying attention. In how many other areas of your life are you currently looking in the wrong places for the right solutions? How many other channels are you on… and receiving only a sea of static? How many more days, months, weeks, and years will you sit and say, "Maybe tomorrow; maybe things will change tomorrow." Tomorrow is literally a figment of your imagination. Your *life*, on the other hand, is a very real part of today.

TIME IS MONEY

Notwithstanding the afore-listed monetary aspects of the cost of a television, the greatest cost attributable to your television is the cost of your time.

How much money do you earn an hour? If you were the boss, and your paycheck was paid in units of time, how much would you pay yourself per hour? Remember: time cannot be manufactured. Time will never be made; it can only be measured in quantities of twenty four hours per day.

For every hour you spend watching television, you will forever lose two full hours of "doing something else." Allow me to explain. Most of the programming on television is a vast wasteland. Thus, the first hour you potentially lose is the hour spent watching a program that will probably add little or no value to your life.

Then there is the second hour. Ultimately, there are things at home that absolutely need to be completed. However, because we tend to see our lives as infinite, we tend to procrastinate and delay doing the things we simply have to do. Ultimately, you will spend additional time (say an hour) completing a task that could have been completed while you were watching television. Thus, you now have a net loss of two full hours. Imagine this simple example extrapolated over the course of a few months or several years. How much time have you lost? Now, I realize that this example may appear to be only a conceptual theory. However, in a very real way, this is how our lives can be affected by television.

Without a doubt, there are some great programs available on television. The Public Broadcast System (PBS) has superlative shows that can enrich your evening, teach your youngsters, and open up a whole new world for you and your family.

Oprah Winfrey continues to change the landscape of talk-show television while educating untold numbers of women and men on topics ranging from abandonment to zippers. And with cable companies continually changing their available lineups, there is certainly more quality television content today than there was just a few years ago. The challenge is to find a good catch amid a sea of mindless babble. Interestingly, we pay attention to the programs on television, without paying attention to the amount of time spent watching those programs.

TRUE CHANGE OCCURS NOW

At this point in the book, I extend a wonderful challenge to you: over the next two weeks, make a concerted effort to become keenly aware of all the fabricated, divisive, or unusually negative information that tends to inundate your world on a daily basis, especially on the evening news. Remember: you have a very finite attention span.

Once your attentiveness is saturated, your receptors begin to shut down. Like a savings account rapidly approaching a zero balance, your mind can only handle a limited amount of input and output. After you have paid out so much attention, your mind begins to lose focus, and you literally need to rest your thoughts. If you don't rest your thoughts, your mind will soon start to wander, daydreaming as it tries to take short, quick naps.

We often begin the day with great energy and the greatest intentions. Whether turning over a new leaf or simply trying to be nice to everyone we see, many of us attempt to make the most of our day. However, after a few headlines of the local or national newspaper, our attention is lowered to a decreased state of positivism. During the ride or drive to work, the talk radio stations assail our ears as the commentators spew vicious venom to anyone willing to *pay* attention. Believe me: it is very expensive to listen to the diatribe dripping from those felonious radio waves. A significant price is paid as your inner thoughts conform to the thoughts and ideas being loosed into your mind. Country and Western, Rhythm and Blues, Acid Rock... spend a few minutes and really *listen* to the words entering your mind. Ultimately, when you learn a song, your mind permanently plants those words in the far recesses of your mind. Perhaps this is okay for a great love song. However, a large portion of today's songs are about loss, pride, and lost pride.

If you happen to miss the opportunity to spend/waste your allotted attention on the radio tirades, feel free to glance at any of the ubiquitously placed television screens available any and everywhere.

Virtually every public place clamors for your attention. And like the overdrawn bank account that rejects any additional withdrawals, by the time you have finished *paying* attention to other people, places, events, songs, magazines, signs, menus, projects, and other "*very important*" things, you won't have any attention left for the most important person in the whole world: you.

Thus, I challenge you to make a concerted effort to catch yourself watching (*paying attention to*) television's simplistic, condescending shows. And when interacting with people, I dare you to count the number of times you encounter negative remarks when someone could have provided a more positive image to your world.

Furthermore, I dare you to invert all negativity by 1) refusing to get off on that Elevator floor, and 2) responding to any negative remark with a strong sense of positive energy. I dare you to make people pay attention to your newfound positive demeanor.

PAY YOURSELF FIRST

A good financial advisor will tell you that a successful investment strategy starts with the premise to *pay yourself first*. Before you spend any money on bills, gifts, or toys, make sure you set aside a small amount of money for your personal savings account.

By paying your savings account first, you are choosing to prioritize your spending habits. You are creating a secure financial future; making it a high priority in your financial life. Likewise, when it comes to paying attention, start with the promise to pay yourself first. Don't wait to see how much attention is remaining at the end of the day; pay yourself first! By paying attention to yourself first, *your* time becomes the priority.

Your time is a commodity worth much more than money. You can always earn more money, and when your financial account is low on funds, a line of credit is usually not too far away.

Time, on the other hand, is right here, right now... and never again. And, unlike money and credit, you simply cannot borrow more time.

Get up every day; call and face the Elevator of Your Mind; and press the "up" button. Stay on your personal Elevator until you ascend to the proper floor of your destination. Do not allow other people, places, or things to steal your attention. Do not allow other people to convince you to exit onto floors which will only harm you or someone else. Share your little "No Negativity" sign. Make other people earn your attention, and always remember that your allotment of attention is truly limited... it is not infinitely available to everyone who wants a piece of you.

And finally, remember this: You are extending trust every time you open a book, read an article, watch a movie, or simply engage in seemingly pointless conversation. Be careful with where you place your trust. Trust in today; for tomorrow is only a figment of your imagination...

How much time is remaining in your life account?

7: Overdrawn

As a military officer, my professional activities extend into my personal life. When I was assigned to the submarine, for example, my place of employment was an enormous steel tube that weighed over 6,000 tons. While deployed on a particular mission at sea (in the sea, under the sea), I  worked, ate, and slept, onboard the submarine. And though the living conditions have improved immensely onboard today's technologically advanced submarines, time spent on deployment is time spent away from family and friends. Indeed, a whole new standard of living begins to take effect when submariners take to the sea.

The hull of a submarine needs to be especially strong to withstand the tremendous pressures of the deep ocean. Thus, there are no windows... and the sun is no longer visible to help the human body understand the difference between day and night. Instead, the all-male crew works in a typical 18-hour day. Six hours are spent "standing duty," and the other eighteen hours are split between six or seven hours of working on one's primary job, and the remaining time is spent sleeping. Standing duty or "*watch*" is a non-negotiable requirement onboard a United States Navy submarine.

In addition to having a primary job, submariners also stand watch at various shipboard stations, monitoring electrical and mechanical systems and ensuring the safe operation of the ship. Thus, a highly-trained technician may spend seven or eight hours performing preventive or corrective maintenance on equipment... and subsequently spend another six hours monitoring similar equipment while standing watch.

Of course, there is time allotted for sleeping and eating. But, for the most part, there is not much fun time at sea. Because of the long, arduous workdays, when it's time to hit the rack, sleep arrives quickly. Because of the sub's stealthy mission, and because everyone values his own sleep time, maintaining a quiet demeanor in the berthing area is seldom problematic.

Long work days are punctuated with some of the best food in the Navy. Some submarines have specific theme meals planned and designated on particular days of the week. Taco Tuesday, Fish Friday, and Spaghetti Saturday are all popular adaptations of themed meal nights. The best theme meal, however, is reserved for the night before return to port (RTP). The night before RTP is always Pizza Night.

When I was assigned to the submarine, I was intrigued by the sheer irony of the daily life onboard a nuclear-powered submarine. It is ironic that the Sailor's separation from family is as stark and sudden as is the time-honored integration of professionalism and close-knit camaraderie among the crew.

The isolation from family can be brutal; thus the crewmembers often immerse themselves in work, seeking a mental distance commensurate with the geographic space soon separating Sailor from spouse, father from child, and men from their shore-based lives.

The irony is also reflected in the shift of perceptions related to time. Indeed, the sun still shines above the shimmering sea; but deep beneath the towering waves, the submarine and her crew steer quietly through the darkness of the depths; navigating through an entirely different world. In the submariner's world, one knows what time it is; but not what *time of day* it is... a subtle but certain difference. In the submariner's world, days are shorter, and the nights are equally short. In fact, there simply is no day or night... only time.

When at sea, I often found myself thinking and dreaming about events, opportunities, and actions that I wanted to do, but was precluded from doing because of the limited space onboard a submarine. As indicated in previous chapters of this book, I was an avid runner – but not while traversing the depths of the Pacific Ocean. I was also an energetic chef (or so I thought) – but not while sitting at periscope depth off the coast (of an unnamed country). Similarly, I was an engaging son, a communicative father, and a favored friend who enjoyed the companionship of my then-girlfriend (now-my-wife), Delia. But, alas, all those personal characteristics did not necessarily apply while I was deployed on the submarine.

Whenever the submarine negotiated the deep waters of the Pacific Ocean, the watch standers in the sonar room stood a vigilant watch, ensuring we did not crash into ships, boats, or other submarines (there are a few others out there). Some watch standers were actually engaged in "driving" the submarine; others were responsible for cooking the meals. And yet, others were in charge of managing spare parts for the multiple electronic systems used to navigate the submarine through the open seas. Every single person on the nuclear-powered submarine has multiple jobs; and each job is of equal importance. Without the cook, the crew does not eat. Without the radiomen, all communication is lost. And without a complete effort from each man, the synergies of the crew do not exist. Every man is important. And back at home, every man is truly missed.

From the time the men depart the fading dock, every Sailor patiently awaits his return to the family and to his friends missing him ashore. The initial hours after departure are spent rigging the ship for dive; then rigging the ship for sea. Then, the hours fold into days; the days into weeks; and the weeks into long, interesting months. Though days, weeks, and perhaps months away, the return to port is thought of fondly, but not often. The men soon make the transition from family man to fighting man. Sailors don't *fight* in the traditional sense of Army men; Sailors fight the potential ravages of the sea. For a submariner, two of the greatest threats include fire and flooding.

Take your pick; which of the two would you rather face on a submerged ship, hundreds of feet beneath the surface of the ocean? Fires are especially dangerous because the smoke can permeate areas of the ship that are remotely distant from the fire. Because of superior technological advances, today's nuclear-powered submarine creates its own fuel; it also maintains a complete self-contained ecosystem and atmospheric balance, without surfacing for air.

In fact, food is the only limiting factor in today's nuclear-powered submarines (aside from mechanical failure). However, the elaborate maze of supply-and-return ventilation systems also provides a perfect conduit for thick, acrid poisonous smoke (a common by-product of electrical-mechanical fires). Thus, even if Sailors are several compartments away from a main-space fire, the resultant smoke can kill the most resilient of men.

Perhaps equally frightening, flooding is the danger most closely associated with sea-going vessels. Because the submarine is a submerged vessel, it encounters significantly more risk than a surface ship. At five hundred feet below the surface of the ocean, the sea water exerts enormous pressure on the hull. In fact, when a submarine makes a rapid descent into the ocean depths, the crew can actually hear hull-popping noises as the hull of the submarine compresses from the tremendous pressure. The tiniest of holes in the submarine's hull would, indeed, be catastrophic. However, there are also hundreds of interior valves, pipes, flanges, and other associated equipment that can potentially spring a leak.

Because of the potentially deadly nature of fires and flooding, submarine crews train incessantly... constantly monitoring, evaluating, and reviewing several types of drills. Flooding in the engine room; flooding in the crew's mess; fire in the galley; fire in control (where the helmsmen/sub drivers sit)... multiple scenarios are considered. And for the most part, the drills are complex scenarios, requiring multitasking thoughts, plans, actions, and continuous assessments and reporting. There are injuries to attend; reports to make (to the commanding officer); decisions to be made; and personnel to direct... and then there is the catastrophe itself. All these events and actions must be completed in a near-perfect response. In a catastrophic event, anything less than a near-perfect response will garner serious injury or death to the crew.

The submarine *USS SAN FRANCISCO (SSN 711)* faced just such a disaster when it slammed into an undersea mountain at over 25 knots (nautical miles per hour) while transiting to Brisbane, Australia on January 8, 2005. The high-speed impact killed one Sailor and caused severe injuries to another twenty-four service members. As you can imagine, there was a very real sense of terror on the submarine. The collision was not a drill; it was the real thing. And despite numerous injuries, the crew responded heroically, saving the submarine and, more importantly, saving their very own lives. Unfortunately, one Sailor later died from injuries sustained in the crash.[3]

The Sailors of your Navy do not receive huge salaries for risking their lives to protect your freedom...

They know, understand, and accept that they will not likely get rich while serving on the various ships, submarines, and shore stations around the globe. They also understand and accept the danger that is inherent in completing the missions on our nation's aircraft carriers, destroyers, support ships, and, yes, submarines. Accordingly, prior to departing for a six-month deployment, many Sailors update their life insurance documents, powers of attorney, and their respective wills.

The events aboard the *USS SAN FRANCISCO* serve as a reminder that there are many submariners on "permanent patrol" of our nation's waterways. Not every Sailor returns to port. Spouses of deploying Sailors have to ensure all financial matters are discussed and understood. And since the Sailor is often the main breadwinner for the family, when he departs for yet another deployment, sometimes the finances can get a bit jumbled, especially when a checking account is shared.

Today's information technology facilitates instantaneous crediting and debiting of financial accounts. Electronic debit cards are a viable payment option for goods and services in today's society; they are also becoming the preferred, if not *only* payment option in some areas of the world. Thus, if a deployed Sailor spends all the family's money before payday, his wife may end up in a financial bind on the other side of the world. Despite all of the cash inside, ATM's do not dispense an unlimited amount of money! Withdrawals are limited to the amount of funds actually deposited into your specific checking or savings account.

~ 86,400 ~

Wouldn't it be great if ATMs did, indeed, dispense an unlimited amount of cash? Wouldn't it be nice if you had a wealthy relative who consistently filled up your ATM accounts? Imagine for a minute that you really do have a rich relative. And from the time you were a child, he has given you an ATM account, allowing you to withdraw $86,400 every day... for as long as you can remember.

Given that you are a smart, well-meaning person, you have consistently sent thank-you cards on various holidays. Sometimes you have sent cards "just because." As a recipient of this wonderful gift your entire life, you have absolutely no reason to believe this rich relative would *ever* stop giving you $86,400 every day... for the remaining years of your life.

But what happens when you go to the ATM to withdraw your $86,400, and you find the account closed? Empty. Overdrawn. Closed. Wow... your lifetime ATM account is closed. But was it really *your* account?

Oh, sure, you were enjoying the benefits of having the money passed through the account (the free money; the free lifestyle; and the freedom from thinking about the possibility that the withdrawals could or would ever stop). However, the account was never really yours. All you really ever owned was you. But, if you think about it...

...if you don't control your heartbeat, do you own you?

You... You are special and unique. And you are not average. You are not below average; you are not above average. You are wonderfully blessed. And although you may or may not have a rich relative, you do have the wealthiest Father in the world. And... it gets better! He has stocked your ATM with 86,400 **seconds**.

Yes, every day, you can withdraw 86,400 **seconds** from the "ATM of Life." There are 60 seconds in a minute; 3600 seconds in an hour; and 86,400 seconds in a day. Thus, you are blessed with something far more valuable than money; you have the gift of time. And when harnessed by the wonderfully gifted person that is you, time becomes a tool that is more valuable than the prettiest diamond; more useful than the handiest device; and, sadly, more scarce than either.

Yet... you (*yes you*) waste so much of your time. Your time is here while you are reading these profound words. But it is also there when you defile yourself by watching the nightly news; it is there when you spend too much of it idolizing things and people that simply do not deserve one single second of *your most precious resource*. What will you spend *your* seconds on? (Remember; your account could be closed tomorrow).

Let's look at the time/money similarities.

You pay to put gas in your car, or you pay to use public transportation. The price for a tank of gas, or the fare for a ride on the bus is far cheaper than the cost of the time you *spend* on unnecessary diversions of your life's allotment of minutes, hours, and days. Allow me to explain. A tank full of gas is a tangible, useful product.

A ride on the bus provides a tangible, useful service: a mode of transportation. These are good uses of money.

But take a minute and consider what you are getting in exchange for your (wasted) attention? As you will soon see, you are paying far too much (attention) on things that are absolutely worthless.

Interestingly, the time/money analogy flows all the way through. In this attention-starved world, we are all living way beyond our current means. We spend attention on people at work, cars on the roads, signs on the street; songs in our heads; commercials in between; magazines; newspapers; neighbors; junk mail; and (fill in the blank here: _____).

Think about it... our time budget is firmly fixed at a budgeted amount: twenty-four hours every single day of every single year. We will never get one more hour, one more minute, or even one more second. And even if we could somehow gain a bit more time, we would probably squander those minutes away as well. Unfortunately, our current lifestyles reflect an almost bankrupt, cavalier attitude toward the limited time we have *now*. Thus, we would most likely misuse whatever else we were given.

It's time to pay attention to what I am saying. You can't borrow from yesterday or tomorrow. All you have is today. What will you spend your attention on today? Think about your answer... *before* your account is closed.

There is **A**lways **T**omorrow... **M**aybe.

8: Are You Above Average?

Let's discuss the concept of averages. Take a guess at the answers to the following questions:

- How many times a *day* does the average couple have sex?
- How many times a *week* does the average couple have sex?
- How many times a year does the average couple *argue*?
- How much money does the average couple spend on food?
- What is the normal temperature for Phoenix?
- What is the average temperature for Baltimore?

We see the phrase "normal temperature" frequently discussed on the evening news. But, in reality, what is considered "news" to "them" is not necessarily news to you. What is a "normal" temperature? Moreover, what is an average or normal couple?

Your local news may interchange the two words (normal and average); but the two words should really mean absolutely nothing to you. After all, what is the *average* ethnicity in the United States? What is the *normal* dinner? What is the *average* car? What does the average person do on an average day?

Give these seemingly mundane questions some thought, and ask yourself, "Am I secretly comparing myself to the average person?" If you are, indeed, comparing yourself to the average person (and I think most people do), you are selling yourself extremely short.

Your relative worth is measured by your relatives...
not by the piles of stuff you have
relative to your neighbors.

This is an obvious play on words, but the point is clear: use the word *relative* to describe people to whom you are related. As a person, you do not have *relative worth*; you are wonderfully irreplaceable. And if you feel the urge to compare yourself to something, compare yourself to the best that you can do. It is far too easy to compare yourself to the average person. Likewise, it's even easier to conquer the average person.

Why?

Because the ***average*** person doesn't exist!

The real challenge is to be the best person you can possibly be. An even greater challenge is to start the path to being that (best) person *today*. Next week may never come. Don't wait until tomorrow; don't assume you have another hour to plan, procrastinate, or promise yourself or others that you will change into a new person.

Your time has come; all your dreams are on their way.[4]
You are not average; you are a special, unique creation.

God Himself
has breathed life
into the soul
that is you.

Someday, though, your heartbeat *will* stop. Someday, your physical *life* here on earth will meet its own death. The average lifespan is 77.8 years.[5] But remember: you are **not** average. Starting a new life of extreme positivity may seem easier said than done. However, if you are truly ready for a new phase in your life, keep reading. Your solution awaits!

9: Take Me to the Next Phase

As a Supply Officer in the United States Navy, I have been afforded the opportunity to work in a diverse area of operations, including ashore at a Naval Air Station, at sea onboard a large naval ship, and within the sea aboard a nuclear-powered submarine. By far, the tour on the submarine was the most challenging and most rewarding of any assignment (outside of the short stint in Iraq).

As of the printing of this book, the population of the world stands at 6,708,091,817.[6] Less than .001% of the people in the entire world will ever hear the famous submariners' call of *"Dive! Dive!"* Over 99.99% of my earthly neighbors will never have the distinct patriotic pleasure of traveling faster than 25 knots (nautical miles per hour) at depths over 400 feet beneath the surface of the world's oceans (the actual, deeper depth to which a submarine can submerge is classified).

Most people will never see the sunset through the lens of a periscope (not exactly a good thing when it's been several weeks since you last saw sunlight). For the most part, people don't usually get the opportunity to dive into and swim in equatorial waters over 5,000 feet deep.

At the same time, most people don't leave their loved ones for up to six months at a time, deploying to the far reaches of the deepest oceans, and returning again... only to leave again shortly thereafter. In the typical American family, most men are at their wives' side when their children are born.

Most fathers attend their teenagers' graduation.

Most husbands attend their anniversary dinner.

And the vast majority of American men watch at least part of the annual Super Bowl. In the life of a submariner, attendance at many of those events is uncertain and often unlikely. Many of those family-related events go unattended by submariners every year.

In the life of a submariner, the tempestuous sea is where he makes his living. The mighty depths of the world's oceans are where the submariners are serving during many of those momentous family occasions. In fact, the sea is where many submariners have gone on "permanent patrol" while protecting our nation's territorial waters. The safety of our nuclear submarine fleet is unparalleled and unrivaled. Yet, notwithstanding such a profound safety record, the *USS THRESHER* was lost on April 10, 1963, while on sea trials. And the *USS SCORPION* was lost on May 27, 1968, while returning from deployment in the Mediterranean Sea.[7]

And, like my experiences in Iraq, during my assignment as the Supply Officer Department Head onboard a U.S. submarine, I was sometimes troubled by the knowledge that the Navy had previously lost these marvels of engineering might. Because of the crew's professionalism and the submarine's superior technology, I was never fearful for my life. However, the immense supremacy of the ocean is often under-appreciated until you are well within the grips of its incomparable power. Career Sailors grasp this concept quickly, and they learn to respect its awesome power.

In contrast, many of their friends and family simply can't quite comprehend or submit to the idea of getting into a 360-foot-long steel tube, shutting the hatch, and diving several hundred feet beneath the surface of the ocean. As it should be, the U.S. submarine force is an all-volunteer community, and the Navy carefully screens every single applicant, evaluating each Sailor for claustrophobic tendencies and other particular characteristics.

Family members of crewmembers, on the other hand, tend to react wildly different than their well-seasoned, crewmember husbands and sons. Many family members express terror when confronted with the mere thought of traversing through the mighty ocean in a submarine. Imagine the panic they feel when actually onboard the vessel! I witnessed a classic civilian reaction during a one-day cruise in Pearl Harbor, Hawaii.

Every now and then, the United States Navy conducts a one-day family member cruise, allowing the wives, parents, and children of crewmembers to take a short ride out to sea in the submarine on which their proud Sailor is a crewmember. Typically, the four-hour trip includes such momentous events as "angles and dangles" (pitching the submarine at extreme angles fore and aft); a high-speed run (running the submarine at a flank bell); an onboard lunch (literally the best in the Navy); and, the granddaddy of them all: an "emergency blow" (flushing high-pressure air into the ballast tank, forcing the submarine to the surface like a submerged, empty soda bottle popping out of a bathtub).

On this particular occasion, one of the Chief Petty Officers had invited his wife to enjoy the trip. But just as the topside personnel were shutting and locking the hatch, the Chief's wife screamed, *"I can't take it; let me out!"* She stood beneath the escape hatch (exit), shaking her head back and forth while repeating, *"Let me out! Let me out!"* A few of the junior Sailors looked on in disbelief. I quietly explained to them that different people react differently to the closed, submersed environment. Eventually, the Sailors and I digressed into a conversation about innate differences among the wide variety of people in the world. The conversation was interesting, from an academic as well a humanistic point of view.

The young Sailors and I talked about some of the startling differences that exist among the billions of people of this world. Indeed, there is a vast array of spoken and unspoken languages, laughs, and likenesses.

There are innumerable shades of skin color found on every continent. Across this wonderfully small planet, in an infinitely sized world, there are cultures, subcultures, and micro-cultures. Moreover, the path of *your* life differs greatly from the journey traveled by others. Your history is vastly different than that of your parents' past. And if you have children, their world will be significantly different than yours. Despite shared successes and similar backgrounds in education, economics, and ethnicity, you and your closest friends will walk incredibly different past and future paths.

PHASES OF LIFE

Yet, despite the sheer magnitude of the differences existing among you and the other people of Planet Earth, we all share a common path of transition through five basic phases of life:

- *Birth to Brains*
- *Brains to Belonging*
- *Belonging to Bestowing*
- *Bestowing to Bemoaning*
- *Bemoaning to Bygones*

Beginning with birth, we follow the same life trajectory:

- *Birth to Brains:* we learn; and we are educated. First, as babies, and then as school-aged children, the influx of information we receive is simply extraordinary, and our lives are dominated by learning as we flow naturally into the next phase.

- *Brains to Belonging*: we begin to place our accumulated knowledge into a self-reflecting context, seeking understanding, perspective, and order in a world that *appears* riddled with chaos.

- *Belonging to Bestowing*: older and more confident after revamping and refining the beliefs we have thought of as truth, we try to share our knowledge.

- *Bestowing to Bemoaning:* wiser and tested by the mere experience of life, we lament over what could have been if we had the benefit of youth and experience.

- *Bemoaning to Bygones:* in this final phase of life, there is a certain serenity; a gracious quality that is only acquired by years of fears, tears, and passing of peers. As an aside, it should be noted that this certain serenity is actually a manifestation of *acceptance*, which, as I discussed in an earlier chapter, is the fundamental key to a changed life.

Each of us, at one time or another, will fall into one of the above categories (provided, of course, we reach the gracious title of Senior Citizenship). Regardless of the country of citizenship, you and every healthy person you know will pass through one of these distinct phases. And though every phase is distinct and separate from the other phases, every period except *"Birth to Brains"* is affected by another era. (We are not responsible for where we were born. And for the most part, we should not be held accountable for *how* we were raised).

The five phases listed above are not categorized by any particular age groups. People learn, mature, and integrate themselves into society at different rates of time. Some guys plant their first kiss in college; other lads fare better far earlier. Some people achieve their own sense of belonging (a relativity factor) at an early age; other people remain conflicted about their identity long into adulthood. In general, though, once a young man reaches the age of twenty five, he should be well on his way to becoming responsible and accountable for himself. Likewise, and not arbitrarily so, by the age of twenty-five, young ladies should have gleaned enough Capital 'T' Truths to begin assembling a path through the phase of *Bestowing*.

What period of life most closely matches your style of living? Perhaps a more relevant question is, "Which phase of life will be your *last* phase?"

If someone were to ask you to predict a timeframe or phase in which you think you will die, you will probably answer by saying you are contemplating an exit "somewhere around the *Bygones* phase."

In reality, though, a sad medical prognosis is pronounced to a family member somewhere, everywhere every minute of every day. As you very well know... people die every hour of every single day.

THE VALLEY

The United States Geological Survey (USGS) recently reported that several million earthquakes take place in the world each year. Many of the tremors go undetected; but approximately fifty earthquakes are recorded each day (about 20,000 a year).[8] Hurricanes, floods, tornados, and many other natural disasters occur quite frequently, some with little or no warning. In 1996, deaths related to automobile accidents occurred at the rate of five per hour in the United States. And if you think you're safe because you don't drive, keep in mind that several thousand of those deaths involved pedestrians and bicyclists.[9]

I could go on and on, delineating the countless ways in which people die every day. However, the horrific events of September 11, 2001, probably provide the best example of how closely death stalks your daily path. Regardless of where you work, what you do, or how you *plan* to die, you simply do not know the date and time when that event will occur.

And, yet, we remain aloof to the fact that the Valley of the Shadow of Death is not some distant desert basin. It's your den, your driveway, and your daily commute. It's your health, your home, and your honest neighborhood. The Valley of the Shadow of Death is right here, right now. And *pretending* that The Valley doesn't exist... does not change the Truth of its existence.

In other words, ignoring the prospect, probability, and absolute assuredness of your death does not decrease the likelihood that you will die. Regardless of which phase you are in... and irrespective of which phase of life you *plan* to die, you may very well find out tonight if there is life after death.

In Chapter 6, *"May I have Your Attention Please,"* I discuss the concept of perspectives and how our very own view of the world can actually be very wrong. Specifically, on Page 70, you may recall the example of my wife's view of the gas gauge, and how she erroneously believes the car is almost out of gas. Well, here's a question for you: *As the driver of your car... or the leader of your life... when will **you** run out of fuel?* Regardless of what your specific gauges or views are telling you, only God knows the Truth. Thus, if you have very little control over the timing of your last heartbeat, does the beating heart really belong to you? Or is it...

God's Heartbeat?

10: Ingredients of Great Leadership

Leadership. Why is an accurate definition of this particular word so elusive? Throughout my career as a Naval Officer, I have met several inspirational men and women in positions of authority. But the vast majority of them simply were not effective leaders. Did they lead people and manage organizations? Of course they did. And if you ask them, they will probably tell you their *positional* leadership is all that matters.

Yet, ask them to provide a true definition of leadership, and most will recoil into the far corners of their minds, seeking a long-lost entry from a textbook they read many years ago. Indeed, different textbooks provide different definitions of leadership. Consequently, people who study those textbooks often find themselves at odds with other people who have read other books stating different definitions of leadership. But why is a good definition of leadership important to you? As a non-military citizen why should you care about leadership?

*As the leader of your life, you absolutely **must** take the time to understand the baseline contributors to your decision-making process.*

I have heard some people profess, "There is no such thing as 'bad' leadership." I suppose this is a true statement inasmuch as "One man's trash is another man's treasure." However, I strongly oppose the school of thought that states, "There is no bad leadership."

The mere definition of leadership can be quite controversial, primarily because of the subjective nature of the endless assortment of management principles. However, a successful manager is not necessarily a good leader. President William Jefferson Clinton was a successful president; but I would not espouse his ethical conduct as reflective of good leadership. President George W. Bush, like Bill Clinton, was a state governor and then president of the United States. Was he a good leader? Did he have good leadership qualities? That's a question best answered by historians. Both Clinton and Bush, as commanders-in-chief, were leaders. However, their style of leadership varied greatly.

Likewise, other leaders can apply a vast array of different principles when leading people through various situations. And because everyone sees the world as a little bit (or greatly) different than the next person, a great leader has to have significant insight into the various opposing viewpoints existing in his or her organized unit. Those different viewpoints are often based on and reflected in the differences in ethical values that exist in different people. And, though seemingly small, those differences in ethical principles can actually reflect deep chasms of divergence; points of position far apart from each other in scope and depth.

And, since many leadership styles advocate a certain sense of integrity or moral responsibility, most principles of leadership center around religion, politics, or some other potentially divisive concept. Some leadership ideals appear superficially straightforward and simple (i.e. "do the right thing"), while others are deeply rooted in culture, tradition, or other esoteric characteristics. Still, *successful* leadership is not always *good* leadership.

THE *CLARK MODEL OF LIFE LEADERSHIP*

Based on the premise that ***perceptions matter*** more than anything else, the *Clark Model* is actually a cyclical, self-sustaining loop. The *Clark Model* is expressly based on the premise that there are at least three ways to view life:

1. The way you see it;
2. The way others see it; and
3. The way things really are; the Capital 'T' Truth

At any given time, these three points of view can be totally aligned or entirely misaligned. In other words, your perception is usually different than another's observations. And because of the vast differences in perception, your perceived reality may be closer to the Capital 'T' Truth; while another's point of view more closely aligned with fantasy.

Rarer still are the unlikely events that all three perspectives are in perfect alignment... or that all three (perceptions and reality) are mutually exclusive.

An excellent example can be seen in various aspects of life. Employers have numerous expectations for their employees, but some employee/employer relationships are doomed from the beginning, simply because the employee's idea of a successful, productive workday is far different than the employer's definition of a great workday. In this example, please note the two perspectives from which each person thinks. The Truth exists somewhere in between their respective beliefs. Likewise, the husband/wife, parent/child, teacher/student, and every other relationship dabbles a bit in the Truth... and a bit more in the untruth.

Perceptions and perspectives, however, in and of themselves, are not a true reality. In your mind, you may *feel* something to be true. But, in reality, it's all in your mind. Yes, the thought *does* exist in your mind; thus, the thought truly *does* exist. But, to be a (Capital 'T') Truth, your perspective must incorporate more than mere feelings. Your perspective must have **context**.

The *Clark Model of Life Leadership*
is purely contextual and is based on a
Self-Awareness Situational Assessment Loop

That's a fancy title for saying the following:

By taking the time to study your literal
self, you will come to know yourself.
(Self-awareness)

However, you must realize that your 'self'
changes, depending on the situation.
(Situational)

Thus, you must continuously assess your
self, environment, and mission... as well
as the dynamics occurring when any of
these items independently changes.
(Assessment)

And, considering the constantly changing
details of your environment, you must
continuously assess how those (new)
changes affect you and your mission.
(Loop)

The *Self-Awareness Situational Assessment Loop*
identifies three key humanistic behaviors that define *who*
we are and *how* we see the world. Each individual
humanistic behavior provides significant momentum and
structure to the other two processes. Thus each behavior
tends to promote and prosper (or degrade and degenerate)
from the other two behaviors. This super-integrated blend
of actions and decisions is either a fantastic force helping
you to easily adapt to a dynamic landscape; or it is a
horrific harness keeping you exactly where you are.

This super-integrated blend of actions and decisions ultimately creates a powerful thrust towards continuous change. Or, on the other hand, this blend of actions works to prevent you from succeeding at any attempt to amend, adjust, or revitalize any part of your One True Self.

In other words, to truly change, you must address all three key areas of your life: *priorities*; *presentations* (perspectives); and *propensities* (your habits).

Why are these concepts extremely important in the context of life leadership? The answer is in the question.

Leadership is entirely, unequivocally, and "*unforgivingly*" contextual. Great leaders understand the concept of the *moment of leadership*; and that it is not really a moment, but rather a continuum. The moment of leadership is not a position to be held, but rather a place in time. We can all be leaders, but most people will never be great leaders. Why not? Because most people simply don't want to spend the effort needed to process the vast array of real-time information in a given leadership scenario. Moreover, most people don't understand the intricate, powerfully strong integration of priorities, presentations, and propensities. The following pages will provide significant insight on how these three areas affect you and your life.

*What are **your** specific*
priorities, presentations, and propensities?

ACADEMICALLY SPEAKING

I'd like to keep this chapter fairly straightforward. My intent is to provide an understanding of the three powerful forces keeping you on your *current* path. This is the only academic portion of the book. And, though the concepts may initially appear challenging or difficult to understand, please take your time and slowly absorb the material.

If you begin to feel intimidated by the material, simply skip to Chapter 13, *"Choose Your Superlative."* You can always come back to Chapters 10-12 later.

As you begin to grasp the importance of the three individual parts of the model, take time to understand the exponential importance of the most important aspect of the model: the loop connecting the three components of priorities, presentations, and propensities. If necessary, refer back to the various pictures of the loop. After gaining an understanding of the *Self-Awareness Situational Assessment Loop,* you will be able to clearly see why you do the things you do. More importantly, you will gain a whole, new perspective.

Remember: leadership is entirely, unequivocally, and **unforgivingly contextual.**

As the leader of your life, you absolutely must *take the time to understand the baseline contributors to your decision-making process.*

ESSENTIAL INGREDIENTS OF LEADERSHIP

If you are a leader in an organization (work, family, etc.), the *Self-Awareness Situational Assessment Loop* can be a powerful tool in helping you and others discuss, define, and refine your respective priorities, presentations, and propensities. We are all leaders of our own specific life.

As I discussed earlier, employee and employer expectations often differ greatly. Parents and children often see the world from two entirely different perspectives. Yet, in the midst of the differing points of view, a True and accurate (point of) view does, indeed, exist. Perhaps the employee is correct when he perceives a good days work as "eight hours at the office." Or maybe the employer is *more* correct when she sees a good day's work as something more meaningful and more tangible... a completed report, an achieved goal, or a finished product. Both perspectives are real. As an organizational leader, and as the leader of your specific life, your perspective matters more than anything else. Your perspective affects how you see the world. Your perspective affects your habits. And your habits, your propensity to do certain things, affect how you prioritize the *important things in your life.*

The previous chapters of this book are focused on helping you accept a very important fact about your life here on earth. The fact is: you are closer to death today than you were yesterday. I am not trying to be morbid.

However, the previous chapters of this book are built on a foundation of two very simple concepts: life and death. By accepting the assuredness of death, you can begin to assert a greater appreciation for the finiteness of life. Thus, by gaining an appreciation for death, you will gain an appreciation for life. In Chapter 3, I make a big deal about **choosing** your attitude. As you may recall, I ask you to choose the "up button" every day. Though people may challenge this mentality, you *can* succeed at making every day an "up" day. But it all starts with a choice. Likewise, as you read the next few pages, keep in mind the beauty of seeking one simple item: the Highest Truth. The *Self-Awareness Situational Assessment Loop* will challenge you to reconsider how you **see** the world; it will challenge you to change your thoughts about yourself; and it will lead you to seek a True Truth.

God's Heartbeat is written to help you accept a few basic points of life (many points we know to be true, yet we consciously ignore). *God's Heartbeat* is not so much about being happy as it is about helping you to see that **man's view is always flawed**; God's view is always perfect. *God's Heartbeat* is all about educating you on how our perspectives (our presentations) are purely man-made. Indeed, the very title of this book is focused on helping you to see that your life already belongs to God; you just need to accept this Truth before you truly see and adapt to it. Comprised of priorities, presentations, and propensities, the *Self-Awareness Situational Assessment Loop* explains how these items affect yourself (your "self"), environment, and mission.

1. ***Prioritization*** *(Priorities)*
    - Which of these items are most or more important? Rank their relative importance:
        i. Self
        ii. Environment
        iii. Mission

2. ***Presentation*** *(Perspectives)*
    - Assess how your filters (beliefs and upbringing) affect how you present your:
        i. Self to self
        ii. Self to the environment
        iii. Environment to self

3. ***Propensity*** *(Habits)*
    - Realize how habits dominate your beliefs, lifestyle, and potential for change; your specific habits are:
        i. Formed yet entirely changeable (dynamic)
        ii. Passively aggressive
        iii. Fuel for your current priorities, presentations, future propensities

(Copyright 2008 by John H. Clark, III)

Remember: Perceptions are not necessarily reality; they are based on a multitude of influential events, people, places, and self-sustaining beliefs that have slowly integrated their way into the manifestation that is you. *When you change your perceptions, you will change you.*

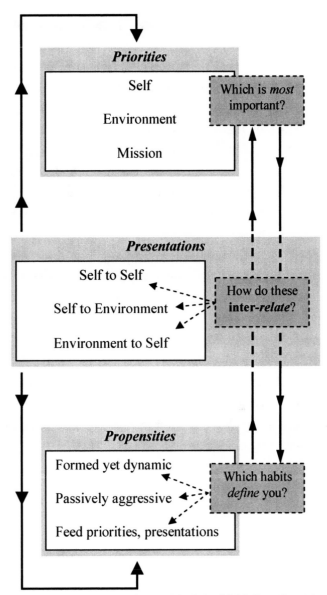

Figure 6: The Clark Model of Life Leadership

(Copyright 2008 by John H. Clark, III)

The three elements of priorities, presentations, and propensities are incalculably dynamic and, at times, interdependent. They are incalculably dynamic because, every second in time is different than the previous point in time. Thus, a walk through a busy intersection garners different priorities than a stroll through a park. This is an obvious contrast. But the point is clear: your priorities change when your environment changes. And in any given situation, you are subconsciously deciding the relative importance of your self, your environment, or the mission in which you are involved.

Don't confuse the word "mission" as a strictly-military application. Your **mission** could be a quick trip to the local grocery store to get a gallon of milk. However, if the local store is being robbed, the importance of your **environment** vaults to the head of the line, only to be overtaken by the importance of your **self**.

In a later chapter, I will focus exclusively on presentations. However, as an introduction, please note [from Figure (6)], there are three specific components affecting our view of an ever-changing world:

1. How we see ourselves
   - *(self to self)*

2. How we present ourselves to the world
   - *(self to environment)*

3. How we see the world
   - *(environment to self)*

Read the next two pages very slowly...

Our presentations change, depending on a multitude of factors. When you feel good about yourself, you probably feel better toward others. Thus, by presenting a good attitude to your self, you will most likely present a good attitude to your environment.

Of course, the converse is usually true as well. When you feel bad about your self, you are likely to share that information by way of a bad attitude, somber behavior, or just plain ol' meanness. As a result, your presentation of your self to yourself (how you *see* yourself) affects you and your environment. For example, many Americans are obsessed with weight-gain. Some already-thin people still believe they are too fat.

And since everyone lives by the same natural laws as you, their "selfs" actually affect **you** (as an actual part of your environment). As you can see, your filters and actions affect how you present yourself to your self. Your filters and actions also affect how you present your self to the environment. And your filters and actions affect how you present the environment to your self.

The last of the three key areas is *propensities.* These are the habits and lifestyles that seem to keep you on the path you currently walk. Your daily routines actually work to prevent you from changing anything in your highly patterned life. Your life of today is indeed patterned after your life of yesterday. Yet, yesterday does not really exist; it is only a memory, a thought, a place somewhere in your mind.

Additionally, your **propensity** to do certain things feeds directly into your **priorities** in life. Whatever you did yesterday and the day before will usually affect what you do today and tomorrow. This discussion on propensities and habits may seem common sense or perhaps ridiculously obvious. However, the *Clark Model of Life Leadership* exemplifies the *extent* to which humanistic keys are integrated and, as such, very resistant to change. Changing your **priorities** is relatively easy; changing your **presentations** is a bit more difficult. Changing your **propensities** is a very daunting task.

Changing all three of your aspects in the
Clark Model of Life Leadership
requires superhuman strength.

Changing all three aspects is absolutely, undeniably the *only* way to foster permanent, real change in you. Changing all three aspects of the *Clark Model of Life Leadership* has a profound effect on what type of life you lead. Your life leadership abilities affect how you view, interact, and ultimately affect the world.

But where can you go to find superhuman strength? Who understands you better than any single person? Who knows your weaknesses and strengths better than your mother, your spouse, or anyone you've ever met? Who can perform the miracle of change... regardless of your current situation? Whose perception should you believe? *Upon what view of the world should your view be based?* Whose view is superlative?

The True Owner of your heartbeat can truly change you. This book provides a very viable option for finding superhuman strength. Within the pages of *God's Heartbeat* I am challenging you to accept a much higher calling. I am expecting you to perform the miracle of change by paying attention to the academic and spiritual discussion I have laid out within the previous chapters.

And though this chapter provides an academic insight into understanding how and why your priorities, presentations, and propensities resist and prevent changes in your life, keep in mind that the true power of change resides in your power to choose your style of life.

After reading a bit more information on the *Clark Model of Life Leadership*, you will soon have the intellectual tools to begin the process of ***managing*** the change in your life. However, *managing* change is not the same as *creating* the change. Why is this distinction so important?

Well, remember: change is constant. You are a different person than you were five months ago; and you have certainly changed over the last five years. Thus, change occurs with or without your consent; time moves on, and you move with it.

Wouldn't it be great if you could somehow
make things happen
and not just move along to get along?

Change is constant. You are a different person than you were five months ago; and you have certainly changed over the last five years. Thus, change occurs with or without your consent; time moves on, and you move with it. But wouldn't it be great if you could make things happen, and not just move along to get along?

Yes, you just read the exact same thing twice. But initially your mind was in denial. Initially, your mind tried to make sense of the obvious repetition. Similarly, in your own life, your mind is often in denial when it comes to objectively evaluating the powerful loop existing between your priorities, presentations, and propensities. The loops in your life may be stronger than you; but those loops *can* be broken. Breaking those loops requires strength greater than yours; breaking those loops requires superhuman strength to re-create a new self.

As I have pointed out, change occurs with or without your assistance. Time moves on, and you move right along with it... sometimes changing in ways of which you are not proud. Change is like a huge boulder breaking loose at the top of a fantastic mountain, tumbling down to the valley below, making its mark on everything in its path; unstoppable. Wouldn't it be great if you could harness the true power of change... and make changes to *positively* affect your life? Wouldn't it be great if you could break loose and positively affect the lives of others in an incredible, almost unstoppable way? After reading this book, you will be able to do just that!

11: The Main Ingredient

Now that I have introduced these seemingly complex life leadership ingredients, an obvious question comes to mind: when trying to effect permanent, real change, which of the three key areas is most important? Which area should you focus your efforts, time, and energy?

*Of the three behavioral areas, the most important area is **presentation**.*

The other two areas, prioritization and propensities, matter a great deal. However, presentations are superlative factors that dominate everything else. You *present* yourself to yourself; you *present* your self to the world (environment); and you *present* the world to yourself (via your preconceived notions and through your previously lived and learned experiences). Presentations are the common elements that bring the mission and environment into one place (interdependence). If you can accept reality for what it is, and if you can objectively consider but reject your other unrealistic points of view, you can then begin to work from a position of Truth.

However, if you continue to see, seek, and support a perspective that is different than a Truth-based reality, your efforts at change are based on a fabrication. And everything based on a fabrication is a mere manifestation of that same fabrication. Everything based on a lie will soon logically falter. Buildings, lives, and bridges built on faulty foundations will someday fall. Thus, to avoid future tragedy, absolute Truth should be your yardstick, your benchmark, and your best measure of success.

At the same time, prioritization is very important. And some may argue that, to effect real change, you have to start by changing the prioritization of your self, your environment, and your mission. This may appear to be a logically sound argument. However, changing your priorities and placing yourself at the top of the importance list will not do anything to help you if you continually see things from an improperly *presented* point of view. In fact, if you re-prioritize without first working on your presentations, you will only reinforce the lies that you (already) believe about your self. Moreover, you will become immune to the True realities of your environment and your stated missions. Like the folks on the *Titanic*, you will descend into a pit of entrenched denial that will be almost inescapable if you do not correct your view of your self, your world, and how the two interact. And, as I often tell my wife…

Never underestimate the power of denial.

Why am I spending so much time and effort communicating the importance of presentations? Some people erroneously believe the problems and solutions of their world are "out there." Many people spend an inordinate amount of time trying to control things which are far beyond their control. Some people disregard the superlative power they have within themselves (the one thing you *can* control is yourself). Some people wholeheartedly accept what the world *presents* to them. Many people *pay* far more attention to their *negative thoughts*; and not enough attention to their *positive thoughts*. Try this: over the next few days select a specific person, and make a focused effort to pay positive attention to that person. The results will be startling; you will see exactly how you really do affect the environment.

Remember this:
The environment changes when you enter into it.

Everywhere you go, you literally change the world.

YOUR SIXTH SENSE

But whose world is it? When does *the* world become *your* world? When is your *environment* more important than your *self*? When is the mission paramount? When should you relegate your *self* to the back burner?

The best way to ask and honestly answer these questions is to accurately assess the current environment, of which you are a part. And the only way to accurately assess anything is to receive and recognize stimuli through your six senses:

1. Seeing
2. Touching
3. Hearing
4. Tasting
5. Smelling
6. Perceiving

It is this 6th sense that we must learn to strengthen. For the most part, our sixth sense has been weakened by self, society, and shame. Our physical *self* is in constant conflict with our perceiving, intuitive, spiritual self. Thus, over time, our perceptions (and presentations to self) become blurred by the input from media, television, friends, family, enemies, and, to a certain extent, our very physical feelings about our self.

As a matter of fact, people tend to view their propensities and priorities through their own flawed presentations. Many people are oblivious to many of their very own habits and ridiculous priorities. It is our very own perspective of the world that prevents us from seeing what we absolutely *need* to see. And until we learn to correctly see our presentations (of self, environment, and mission), there is a distinct possibility (and a probability) that we may *never* see what we absolutely **need** to see.

Until we learn to subscribe to a more authoritative perspective of ourselves, we will remain in the same situational funk, regardless of the various remedies we may try.

Right now, to effect true positive change, you need to agree that your view of your environment is, ironically, constrained by your view of the environment. Moreover, your perception of the environment is most likely considerably different than the actual circumstances occurring within the environment. Up until now, you probably have not even considered how dramatically the environment changes when you enter into it.

Yes, your five senses enlighten you about the world. Through sight, we can distinguish the expectations of a raincloud on the horizon, and we can see a car rapidly approaching the intersection. Through touch, we know the tenderness of a hug and the prickliness of a cactus plant. Through hearing, we can be entertained by melodious music, and we can also be startled by unexpected sounds. Through taste, we often enjoy an after-dinner dessert, and we can tell whether the chicken is spicy or sweet. Through smell, we know when the cake is baked, and when the cake has baked too long.

But it is your sixth sense that truly governs your life. It is your *presentation*, your perspective that rules, governs, and guides your propensities and priorities. Ultimately, once you change your presentations, you will change everything else... everything.

You may not think of your current priorities as wrong, wretched, or requiring significant tweaking. For the most part, people believe their current priorities are great... simply because most people don't fully see or compare their existing priorities with a True benchmark. Likewise, you may not believe your habits are affecting other areas of your life... simply because you literally don't see how your propensities are influencing your self in *all* areas of your life, not just the ones you can readily identify. You may have heard the phrase *"the blind leading the blind."* Well, in your own personal mission of life leadership, the very same thing can happen to you. In areas where you are blind, you simply cannot lead. Well, perhaps you *can* lead, but the results will be disastrous.

Like the military commander who is clueless in battlefield leadership, if you are clueless in the skills required to navigate through the hazards of life, you and others in your life will soon face some rather tragic life-leadership-related consequences. If a military leader is blind to the traps, trips, and trickery of the enemy, how can he be expected to successfully lead the troops to success? If you are blind to your own traps, trips, and trickery of self-inflicted denial, how can you be expected to successfully lead yourself through the Valley of the Shadow of Death?

Accordingly, let's continue an analysis of the *Self-Awareness Situational Assessment Loop* by accepting and understanding your greatest personal limitations. You may have an awesome set of priorities; and you may have superb well-thought-out habits.

But if your view of the world is slightly (or greatly) shaded by preconceived notions, beliefs, or teachings, success will always be a relative, moving target. Saddam Hussein was an accomplished head of state, as was Adolph Hitler. These were men of great power and influence. Perhaps their rise to power can be attributed to their *habitual* need for power; or maybe their explosive influence was gained through a lifetime of placing power at the top of their *priority* list. Regardless of their path to power, they truly believed (perceived) that their view of the world was an accurate view.

These men may represent extreme examples of how badly the human perspective can go wrong. However, the folks on the *Titanic* were equally wrong in their environmental perceptions. Teenagers are equally wrong about their invulnerabilities. And adults are similarly wrong in an estimation of their ability to see things for what they are... especially items related to *self*.

Take a look at the *Self-Awareness Situational Assessment Loop* on the next page. You can readily see how propensities and priorities are previewed, viewed, and reviewed through presentations. Unfortunately, propensities and priorities are more likely to be *overlooked* as they pass through the presentations. This *overlooking* is, in effect, a naturally strong form of denial. Unfortunately, the stronger the denial, the more blind we become. Remember: if your view of the world is obstructed, colored, or shaded by anything (beliefs, teachings, etc.), then true success will always be a relative, moving target. Man's view is *always* shaded.

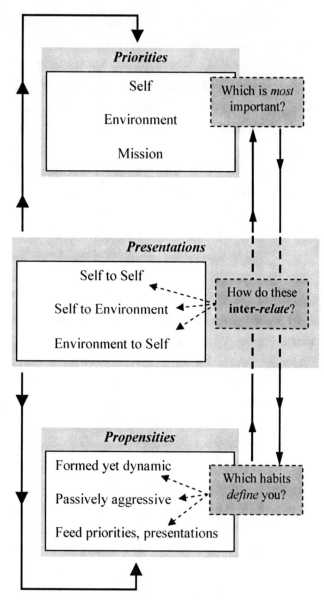

Figure 7: The Clark Model of Life Leadership

Moreover, in a horrific Loop of Ludicrousness, the blinder we become, the deeper our denial digs us into ditches of doubt, danger, and damage.

Regardless of how confident you may feel about your propensities and priorities, to effect true change, you must start with a fresh view of the world. You must shift your current perspective from *your* way to a different way of seeing the world. You already have a point of view... a perspective... a manner in which you present the world to yourself. Your *current* point of view, your *existing* perspective, and the current, existing presentations to self should be **shattered** and then re-created... but from a different perspective; a different presentation.

CHANGE YOUR VIEW; CHANGE YOUR WORLD

Many people don't understand the filters affecting their view of the world. Most people don't understand how their personal actions affect **how** they present themselves to the world. In fact, many people simply don't understand that they, themselves, control their filters, their actions, and their very own world.

Some people simply don't want to hear the Truth.
Some people don't want to hear the simple Truth.
Some people don't want to simply hear the Truth.
Simple people don't want to hear the Truth.

But *you* have obviously made it this far into *God's Heartbeat*; perhaps you are ready for the Truth, the Capital 'T' Truth. If you are interested in seeking Truth, please read on.

Without self and the study of it therein, what is there? Without adequate development of the inner (and outer) being, the other elements of environment and mission are totally disassociated; landscape without throughput, and paint without canvas. Without the captain, there is only the ship tossed upon the waves. Without you, there is only the environment and "stuff" to get done. Thus **you** are the most important aspect of this conversation.

Most importantly, in the context of *presentations*, great leadership requires a near-perfect alignment of presentation of self to self; presentation of self to environment; and presentation of environment to self. These terms may seem confusing. To review, keep in mind the three dynamic (changing) parts of your world:

1. How you see yourself
   - (*self to self*)

2. How you present yourself to the world
   - (*self to environment*)

3. How you see the world
   - (*environment to self*)

Achieving and maintaining a solid alignment of presentations is a very big challenge.
And you ***can*** do it!

When all three facets of presentation are of the same accord, *then* you have the basis for being a great leader. When you achieve this rare feat, *then* you will understand the vast array of information that is comprised of you and your environment... and integrated into you. Only then will you be able to surmise the difference between perception and reality. *Then* you can understand which characteristics affect, promote, and deter real change.

Finally, once you accept and understand the relative importance of your presentations, you can spend more time addressing and changing your perspective... and less time focusing on your priorities and propensities. As I have previously stated, *God's Heartbeat* is not about being happy; it is about helping you to see that man's view is always flawed, and God's view is always perfect. *God's Heartbeat* is all about educating you on how your perspectives (your presentations) are purely man-made. But *there is a Godly perspective.* Once you accept God's perspective and adapt to the effects of today's media-rich environment, you will see that your perspective is under constant, overt attacks to reshape and measure up to a deviously damning man-made view. And, as the leader of your life, you must act now to choose your True Leader and see the world for what it is. Open your spiritual eyes.

12: Superlative Leadership Defined

Some people see things better than other people. And regardless of what one person sees, another person will often *look* at the same thing, yet *see* something totally different. Indeed, perceptions do matter. However, if you **perceive** the water to be 88 degrees Fahrenheit, and, in **reality**, the water is actually *500* degrees 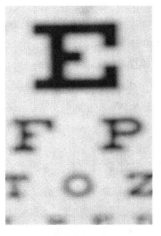 Fahrenheit, does your perception help or hurt you when it's bath time? This is an extreme example, but it is a good example.

To be clear, perceptions exist in three key areas: Perceptions of self; perceptions of environment; and perceptions of mission(s). Each perceived area varies in scope and complexity. Some perceptions are straightforward and easily aligned with Truth (like a boiling bathtub helping you to see that the water is a tad bit too hot for a bath). On the other hand, some perceptions are vehemently defended as Truth, despite the lack of evidence thereof (like the perception that yesterday is more important than today). Self, environment, and mission; these three key perceptions completely dominate the footprint we bring to the world, as well as the likelihood for a successful leadership relationship that is situational, transformational, and principally based.

Moreover, these key perceptional areas make up the heart of mankind. These three perceptional areas drive our associated life-leadership skills. It is the *type* of person that defines and determines the type of leader. Unfortunately, many people believe leadership *ability* is nothing more than leadership *personality* resulting from a leadership *style*. To understand the quality of a person's leadership, you must understand the quality of the person. You must understand how she views herself. You must have an appreciation for her specific presentation of herself to the world. Finally, you must understand how she views the world in which she lives. Perceptions of self, environment, and mission will always drive your priorities and habits.

> *Perceptions about yourself*
> *matter to you because, quite simply...*
> *You believe what you believe.*

Your internal descriptions of self drive your sense of strength, balance, and power – three key ingredients of the successful leadership role. Moreover, your self-confidence is a major factor in defining and redefining who you are and what you hope to achieve. Ironically, a low level of self-confidence does not necessarily relate to a low yield of accomplishments.

The term *Napoleonic Complex,* for example, has been used to describe short men with an insatiable drive to succeed (thus, a person who is self-conscious about his height can still be a super-achiever).

People with a fear of flying have been known to travel the world, albeit via alternative modes of transportation (thus a lack of confidence in flying does not equate to a fear of travel). And yet, those who simply *believe* they cannot achieve certain milestones... are not likely to surprise themselves. The principled point: your internal filters and perceptions drive your very being. Your perceptions define you. If you change your perceptions... *when* you change your perceptions, you will begin to change yourself.

Perceptions of self (self-perceptions) affect the leadership landscape because the role of the leader applying the leadership is tied directly to the goals being set for the leader's subordinates and followers. Each of these components (goal, leader, and follower) is integrated via an application of (the leader's) vision. Consequently, vision matters. *Shared vision* is, almost by definition, an extension of the leader's self. Inventions, innovations, and styles of leadership are all manifestations of inner visions that have been moved from within a person's mind, to the person's environment, sometimes becoming what is known as a shared vision.

Perceptions of the environment matter because the **environment** is the arena in which the characters complete the mission. It is the physical scenery that dots the landscape; it is the organizational structure that confines and allows; it is the unwritten code of conduct that culturally binds and formally chides; it is the path that both leader and follower must take, albeit via different routes. The path *is* shared; the vision *should be* shared.

But it is not the path itself that looms most powerful. It is our *perception* of the path that helps or prevents mission accomplishment. It is your own assessment of the environment, your own *perception* of reality that demands your focus. Additionally, it is your *presentation* of self to the environment that exacerbates or improves your view of both; if you perceive something to be worse than it really is, you have created a different reality. If you perceive something to be better than it is, you have created a different reality. However, your view of the environment is skewed because of the narrow view with which you perceive the environment.

Your view of the environment is skewed because you are an integral part of the environment...

*...an integral part you rarely have an opportunity to accurately see, **unabridged.***

Thus, people often manage themselves with a preconceived, often ill-conceived notion of how they *think* they are in the environment. This is an example of an erroneous self-perception (presentation of self to self). Again, rarely is your assessment of self congruent with reality. In essence, your reiterative self-assessments are an authoritative opponent to change, and a supposition built upon numerous other (incorrect) suppositions.

Many people, unfortunately, rarely *pay attention to* if, how, or *why* their internal assessments are harmonious (or in conflict) with reality.

Such unintended arrogance inevitably leads to a wicked imbalance between the three perceptions of self, environment, and mission.

It is not my intent to prescribe tenets of good leadership. I only seek to delineate the factors that must be infused into the fundamental concept of leading. To that end, the precarious balance of perceptions is very real, regardless of the principles on which these perceptions are based.

In general, *the delicate **balance** between the three perceptions of self, environment, and mission matters significantly more than any one or two of the component perceptions.*

In fact, this **balance** matters more than all three of the individual components. The synergistic aggregation of assessments matters most... assessment of self; assessment of environment; and assessment of mission. When all three assessments are in alignment, there is a solid balance in your life. (See figure 8)

However, if you are incorrect in your assessment and subsequent (mis)application of any component, all three perceptions will be affected, upsetting the *Triangle of Balance*. (See Figure 9) Note that the labels are missing from the unbalanced triangle. This is because, regardless of which assessment is incorrect, all characteristics are affected. Thus, if your assessment of your environment is incorrect, the other two characteristics (mission and self) will be affected.

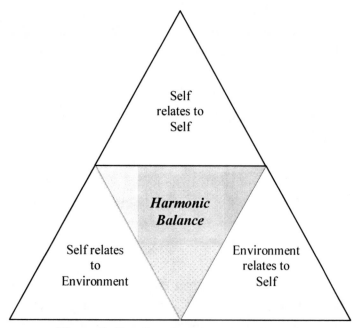

Figure 8: Results of accurate assessments

Only when all three assessments are in balance can there be true harmony. Only then is true great life leadership observed. To what extent a potential imbalance will affect the individual components depends on a variety of factors, specifically the *Self-Awareness Situational Assessment Loop* and your priorities and propensities.

In other words, if at least one of your **perceptions** (self, environment, or mission) is wrong, the other perceptions are also affected. To what extent the others are affected depends on what you value most (priorities) and how you tend to act (propensities).

When you inaccurately assess one or more components...
Everything else is affected. (See Figure 9)

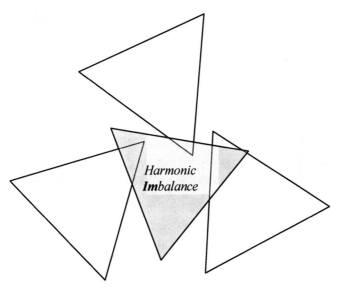

Figure 9: Results of inaccurate assessments

LIFE IS SIMPLE

In fact, one might proclaim that life is painfully simple. We are born, we have needs, and, depending on how and when those needs are satisfied, we simply die. Sure, there is a wealth of activities, events, challenges, and noteworthy causes and effects that punctuate the timeline nestled between birth and death.

But for the most part, our simplistic existence is complicated by pugnacious atrocities called *wants*. These wants are then continuously defined and refined into **perceived** needs. Such a precarious leap of faith from *want* to *need* is the first step in misconstruing a quaint, unassuming, and uncomplicated life into a series of painful lessons about what we need and what we **think** we need... again, an inaccurate *perception*.

So what does this have to do with leadership? Everything. These are not necessarily new life lessons. Self matters... as much as the environment. The enigmas (or missions) we face every minute of every day, in retrospect, are equally important. For example, what is more important: making a left turn or a right turn as you turn onto Main Street while going to work? It depends.

Though the *Self-Awareness Situational Assessment Loop* model is useless without 'self,' greater attention to self is not necessarily tantamount to an increased relevance to or from the same (in other words, paying more attention to yourself does not make you more important to your environment or your given task in life). Remember:

A harmonic balance of
all three (accurate) assessments is what counts.

But what is this balance? Can it help define leadership?

*Can we really define **great** leadership?*

LEADERSHIP DEFINED

Here is where I get technical and academic. Consider yourself well-versed on the *Clark Model of Life Leadership* if you fully understand this brief synopsis of the previous chapters:

> *Achieving balance is feasible only when you have taken an accurate assessment of the aggregated environment. The environment includes you and the changes you have imposed upon the environment by simply being within the environment.*
>
> *True leadership involves...*

1. *Accepting the existence of dynamic interdependencies between yourself, your environment, and your mission...*

2. *Further identifying, understanding, and adapting to those interdependencies; and*

3. *Optimizing the aggregated resources connected to each of those elements... including and* especially *those elements that are created as a result of the absolute aggregation of self, environment, and mission. Great leaders create synergistic energy.*

Aggregating and leveraging created resources is a manifestation of great life leadership. This intellectual and material aggregation is, in effect, doing all you can with all you have; achieving your mission; and actually gaining from all that you have done and are doing.

When you accurately accept and adapt to your inner and outer self, only then will you cease to harbor fallacious views on what is "the right thing to do." Only then can you truthfully say, "I am a great leader."

This would seem to be a great place to end this chapter on leadership. However, before you move on to the next chapter, you must ask yourself one question: *whose perspective* is best? Whose perspective is most accurate? Who is "right"? (See the poem on Page xi.)

Remember: of the three behavioral areas (priorities, presentations, and propensities), presentations (perspectives) matter most. Presentations are superlative factors dominating everything else. Presentations are the common elements bringing the mission and environment into one place (interdependence).

When you accept this profound reality for what it is, you can begin to work from a position of Truth.

However, if you continue to see a perspective that is different than a truth-based reality, your efforts at change are based upon a fabrication (a lie; a fairytale; an unstructured foundation). Everything based upon a fabrication is merely a manifestation of that same lie. Regardless of how great your current efforts and accomplishments may appear, if those achievements are based on a lie, your future feat will surely include a fall.

On the other hand, once you begin to see the world through a True perspective... as soon as you *present the world to yourself* according to the Teachings of God, you will immediately notice a change in your priorities.

As you begin to change your priorities, you will soon see a change in your habits. Once you change your habits (or propensities), priorities, and perspectives (presentations), you are then a changed person. Thus, changing your perspective changes everything else.

Stop working on your habits;
Stop working on your priorities;

Start working on seeing life from the perspective of someone who fears, trusts, and respects...

God

Start living a life for God.

His perspective is superlative.

13: Choose Your Superlative

Have you ever visited a paint store? Have you ever seen the little placards that list all the available colors of paint? The experience can be overwhelming for even the most patient and talented interior designers.

Similarly, your future is a beautiful canvas of unlimited choices, characters, chapters, and changes. But how can you be expected to know which charted path is the best for you? Where can you go to find simple, straightforward advice on life? What is the best way to sift through the multitude of dreams, data, and dabbles of truth? Answers to these questions are not in the media.

In this day and age of overwhelming media, there are so many facets of truth. One advertiser says Brand A is the best choice; while another advertiser spends millions of dollars telling you Brand B is the obvious choice for your money. Indeed, media is everywhere.

I grew up watching commercial media on three television channels. Actually, sometimes our television would draw in a fourth channel if I could convince a sibling or a cousin to hold the TV antennae just right.

Then there was the radio media and its interesting commercials. During my teenage years, television, radio, billboards, magazines, and newspapers rounded out the top five mediums of media. Today, media is everywhere.

In addition to the five venues listed above, media is splashed across buses, barns, and baseball diamonds. At the professional fields there was always media presented; but now you can see media splashed across the high-school and intramural sports fields!

In addition to televisions in employee break rooms, many businesses now have televisions in the lobby. Stores, big and small, provide television-watching as a welcomed alternative to leaving the store earlier than usual. Some families eat their dinner in front of the TV!

As we become more mobile, the availability and integration of media will parallel our increased mobility. Our very own personal cell phones will soon start presenting neat little packets of information for us to attend. And as the personal computer continues its seamless morphing into our lives, media will follow us from home to work, and then back home again. Before departing the office, many people already e-mail homework files to their home computer instead of carrying them home inside a briefcase or satchel. Drivers already use personal navigation devices (PND) to find the best route from Point 'A' to Point 'B'. Many PNDs warn drivers of impending traffic jams and recommend alternate routes. Soon the PNDs may very well advise you of the best place to stop and eat along the way... more media to pay attention.

Along the route to work, there are electronic toll plazas where no money is necessary, as long as your personal electronic account has sufficient funds. At some point, however, as you stop to refuel your vehicle, try not to notice the media begging for your attention at the gas pump. Think about it: before you arrive at your destination, your mind has already made hundreds, if not thousands of decisions on what to do, what to think, and where to go.

I currently work in an office environment located about forty-five minutes from where I live. In the morning, the long commute provides an opportunity to reflect on the day ahead, as well as listen to a few favored Podcasts. On the way home, I use the time to wind down. I usually try to focus on my family, and I try to forget about all the meetings I attended and the numerous e-mails I sent and received throughout the course of the workday. In general, I like the ease of e-mail. It is a great communication medium. In fact, although I have a job as a military professional, I place a unique philosophical quote at the end of every e-mail I send. Regardless of the subject or recipient of my e-mails, I always include one simple directive: *"Choose your superlative; everything else naturally follows."* This tag line is not so much a directive as it is a revelation.

A superlative is something that cannot be toppled. It is the best, the most, highest, the deepest, the longest, and the surest.

Here is the revelation: you make important those things that are important to you. Perhaps this may not sound like much of a revelation. However, many men and women say, "Family is important." Yet they spend all day at work, away from family. Thus, for the guy who spends most of his time at work, family is, relatively and realistically speaking, not really important to him.

Some people say they want to live a healthy lifestyle, yet they do absolutely nothing to advance their style of life in a healthier direction. Thus, the cigarette smoker who spends countless hours inhaling smoke through a paper straw of smoldering, toxic tobacco cannot seriously say that a healthy lifestyle is important to her.

On the other hand, every person is in absolute control over the choices he or she makes in life. As a result, the workaholic can, indeed, change his ways and make his family more important; he can simply curtail his hours at work. Will his wages subsequently decrease? Perhaps; but what is more important, high wages or a loving, close-knit family with a near and dear father?

Long hours at work and a high-paying job are certainly not to be frowned upon. Just don't confuse the high priority of a great salary with the relatively low priority of a greater family. Likewise, those who want a healthier lifestyle can have a healthier lifestyle… if (and only if) they make it important. You are in absolute control over your choices in life.

Decisions are yours alone to make.

Consequently, as I stated earlier, you ***make*** important those things that are important to you. Random things, people, and places are not necessarily important to random people. Indeed, there are some mothers who do not receive Mothers' Day cards from their children. For whatever reason, Mothers Day cards are not important to the children of those mothers. Likewise, there are some children whose healthy lungs are simply not important to their parents who smoke. Oh, sure, the children are important; but the cigarettes are **more** important.

Accordingly, I not only advise you to make important those things which are important, but I also suggest that you ***choose your superlative*** because everything else, by definition, naturally follows. Remember: a superlative is something that cannot be toppled. It is the best, the most, highest, the deepest, the longest, and the surest. Your specific superlative is what you *decide* to put above any and everything else.

Ask yourself, "What choices have I made regarding my first, second, and third priorities in life? Who plays first fiddle in my life? For what person or event do I have the *greatest* respect? Above all else, what matters to me?" **What is your *chosen* superlative?**

In reality, you make conscious and subconscious choices every day. If you have a job, you consciously make the choice to leave your home and go to work; or you decide to stay home. If you drive to work, you may consciously decide to listen to a specific radio station, CD, or audio book. When you eat breakfast, lunch, and dinner, you decide what, when, and where you will eat.

Some may argue that some of these decisions are made for you. Work sites, for example, may offer a cafeteria. Thus, some people would argue that they do not have the choice to eat where they want. However, the existence of the cafeteria does not force you to eat there. Likewise, the mere existence of your job does not command your presence; the music you listen to does not accidentally grasp the inner receptors of your ears. **You** are the only person who decides what **you** do.

Indeed, there are a great many influences affecting you and your life. However, you (your "self") have more to do with your life than anyone or anything else. Regardless of what happened to you yesterday, yester-week, and yester-year, you choose what you will do today. *You* decide which button to push.

*And it **is** just that simple.*

Death, divorce, and dangerous weather conditions can all lead to traumatic, life-changing events. However, as a child of God, you don't have to wait for a huge tragedy to affect your life in a profoundly great way. You can have a life-changing event tonight! Your life-changing event starts with one simple choice: Choose your superlative. Choose *The* Superlative. Seek the knowledge of the One True God; there is no higher form of understanding.

14: Putting it all Together

Now that you have chosen your Superlative, how do you thread together the fabric of change? How does the one simple choice of choosing the correct Superlative... move you to a simple life of serving The Superlative?

Well, the **short** answer is, "One simple choice is followed by another equally simple choice, and then another, and then another..." The **long** answer is discussed in the remaining chapters of this book.

Ultimately, as your days turn into weeks, and the weeks turn into months, your life soon becomes a product of the ensuing results of your collective but singular, simple choices. Like a giant million-piece puzzle that starts at one corner of God's enormous table, your life evolves one piece at a time, one decision at a time, depending on which turn you take: left or right, this or that, these or those, good or bad. Like the elevator door that greets you in any tall building, the Elevator of Life opens to a whole world of subsequent choices and associated decisions.

There are an unlimited number of choices for you to make in your life. There are an infinite number of possibilities that can occur in the next fifteen minutes, fifteen days, and fifteen years.

But, like the elevator door that greets you in any tall building, your ultimate destination depends entirely upon one simple choice. Which "button" will you press as you face your Elevator of Life? Regardless of where you have been; no matter what you have been through.

Yes... Even if you have been "through hell and back," your next step, your *only* step... places you squarely at the front door of the Elevator of Life.

Interestingly enough, if your life has been wonderfully pleasant or perhaps a dream life up until this point, your next step still places you at the front door of the Elevator of Life. In *this* life, there are no guarantees except life and death. You are already in the process of using one of those guarantees; and you simply cannot have life without the *guarantee* of death.

EVERYTHING IS CONNECTED

At this moment in time; this minute; this second; the point in time you are reading these words, the planet Jupiter is lumbering through a gigantic orbit. Earth's orbit is tiny when compared to Jupiter's massive trip around the sun. In fact, while the earth revolves around the sun in a mere 365 days, Jupiter takes 4,330 earth days. Neptune actually takes 165 earth *years* to make one single trip around the sun.[10]

Why does this matter to you? After all, at its closest point Jupiter is 483 million miles from the sun; Neptune is 2.8 **billion** miles from sun. Earth, on the other hand, is only about 93 million miles from the sun. Are you paying attention? Despite the distance from the sun (and us here on earth), if Jupiter were to wobble excessively on its axis or fall out of the sky, the entire solar system would likely explode, implode, or some other type of "plode." In either case, the distance from these celestial bodies does not mitigate the power they have over our lives.

Please notice that I did not say they have a *potential* power over us. I did not say potential power because Jupiter and Neptune have a very real power of connection to your life. And, no, I am not talking about astrology, or whether you are a Capricorn, Taurus, or Leo.

Everything in the universe is connected by a great power.
This connective power is very real.

This power is inescapable; it is powerful; and it affects you every day of your life. You initially noticed this power when you were a child, and you learned very early in life that this power **demands** to be respected. As an adult, you may try to fight the power with all kinds of potions. But alas, this power is all-encompassing. It affects everything from the sun to the planet Pluto... and everything beyond.

I am referring to the power of gravity.

THE POWER OF GRAVITY

Children quickly learn that, as a result of gravity, falling down can be quite painful. Accordingly, little toddlers ultimately learn how to break their fall and land a bit more carefully and softly. Adults see the tangible effects of aging when they look in the mirror and see loose skin. Many people try to prevent the many faces of aging by using cold creams, potions, and abrasion techniques. However, gravity is the main culprit. Gravity pulls and pulls and pulls. It keeps you where you are... as long as you are here on the earth.

If you are above the earth, the forces of gravity will ensure your rightful place back on solid ground. However, gravity is not just an earthly power; it is a celestial power; it is extraterrestrial; it is out of this world. Gravity keeps Jupiter where it is; gravity slings Neptune along its huge orbit around the sun. Gravity is just one of the unseen powers of this world in which we live. Gravity is an awesome power.

But can you see it?

Can you feel it?

Of course not, but you know it's there!

Gravity affects everything and every person.

For this reason, gravity is what scientists call a *natural* law; the Law of Gravitation. And, whether you are a creationist or an evolutionist, you can agree that the Law of Gravitation keeps everything connected. In some strange, inexplicable manner, you are connected to the planet Pluto. Wow!

Again, why does this matter to you?

Well, this little science lesson is not at all about science. This little science lesson is about helping you to see that the world is so much more than media, monkey bars, and monkey liver.

WELL, WHAT DO YA' KNOW?

What do you know about media? I bet you could write a book on the things you see every day: movie stars, household products, upcoming events... to name just a few. What do you know about monkey bars? Well, if you don't know anything about monkey bars, I'll tell you: they are a rather fun (or dangerous) piece of playground equipment for kids (depending on whose *perspective* you choose, the child's or the parent's). Finally, what can you tell me about monkey liver? Is it edible? If it **is** edible, is it tasty?

I sincerely hope you know absolutely nothing about monkey liver. And why would you? You have not paid attention to monkey liver.

However, you may very well know the names of soap opera stars, political pundits, popular restaurants, fantastical movies, and the latest bad news that occurred in your city. Why? You know these bits of information because you probably pay (too much) attention to these types of people, places, and events.

However, if you are already cognizant of the maddening attempt to sap all of your attention; if you have already taken steps to minimize those things that are really not that important, give yourself a pat on the back. You deserve a break today.[11]

If, on the other hand, this concept is entirely new to you... good! *Welcome to a whole new world!* In your new world, which began when you started reading this book, you are (now) the owner and operator of your life. You now realize that there are unseen forces that connect this world to other worlds. Sure, I have only talked about the unseen forces of gravity; but there are a few pages left in this book. And I have saved the best for last.

PUTTING IT ALL TOGETHER

The example about the Law of Gravitation is presented specifically for you to begin the process of wrapping your mind around the concept that there really are unseen forces here in this very real world. Of course, gravity as an unseen force is a relatively easy concept to grasp.

Throw a ball up, and it must come down. Climb a tree, and you'd better be careful. Catch a flight across the country, and you trust the design and manufacturer of the airplane to pay attention to and follow the laws of gravity (Thrust and lift are other unseen forces that are important to airplanes; they are unseen, but very, very real forces). Indeed, our childhood and secondary classes in education taught us about gravity. Many of us were told of Sir Isaac Newton and how his many experiments related to a gravitational force.

However, in reality, you did not really learn the concept of gravity. In reality, you simply *accepted* the concept, *adapted* your thinking processes, and *achieved* an understanding of the mathematical explanation. You *achieved* a certain degree of academic success, depending on how well you accepted the concept, adapted to the model of thinking, and performed on a subsequent academic test.

Again, if you have ever learned about the concept of gravity, you accepted it; you adapted to it; and you achieved an understanding of the concept. But you have never *seen* gravity. Likewise, you have never *seen* love, only a manifestation thereof. You have never *seen* compassion, only an expression of the same.

Furthermore, you have *chosen* to see what you have seen (and how you currently view the world). And you have also *chosen* not to see what you have not seen. This style of living... this *lifestyle* will continue; you will see what you have chosen to see (acceptance), and you will *not* see what you have chosen not to see (denial).

It is now time to change the blind manner in which you have been living. It is time to set aside the beliefs you ***think*** you have. I challenge you to accept the fact that there is an unseen Force in this world.

Whether you are a staunch atheist or a mature Christian, I urge you to make one simple, straightforward choice as you face your Elevator of Life: ask yourself:

DO I BELIEVE IN GOD?

Indeed, *"Do you believe in God?"* is a question.

Yet, the answer you choose to give is based on a choice. And it is **your** choice... no one else can accept the existence of God; you have to do the accepting. No one else can begin to adapt to a life that reflects the teachings of the One True God. Only you can control what you do; thus only you can do the adapting. No one else can make you achieve a universal connection with God and your fellow man, until you accept the teachings, knowledge, and wisdom of God.

Compare your current life path and the associated decisions with the capital letter 'T' and not the capital letter 'Y'. Take a look at the following diagram, and you will clearly see the following description of choices:

Your current path is like the
vertical line of the capital letter 'T'.

Your choices sit at opposite edges of the
horizontal line of the capital letter 'T':
(See Figure 10)

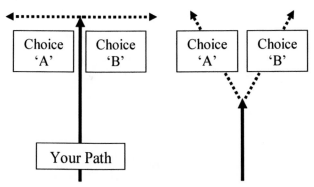

Figure 10: Choices should be compared to 'T' and not 'Y'

There is no proverbial fork in the road. When choosing between a belief and unbelief in the One True God, there is only one decision to be made. The two available choices are directly opposite each other. As you go through life, you are probably paying too much attention to people, places, and things having absolutely no interest in your spiritual growth. Why not pay more attention to the reality of the sheer closeness of your death? Why not embrace the fact that you *will* die?

Why not face the truth that you simply do not know the day, date, or time of your death? And, in fact, *your account dispensing 86,400 seconds daily may be closed tonight.* For it is written in Luke 12:16-21...

The ground of a certain rich man produced a good crop. He thought, "What shall I do? I have no place to store my crops."

Then he said, "This is what I'll do. I will tear down my barns and build bigger ones, and there I will store all my grain and my goods. And I'll say to myself, 'You have plenty of good things laid up for many years.

Take life easy; eat, drink and be merry.'"

But God said to him, "You fool! This very night your life will be demanded from you. Then who will get what you have prepared for yourself?" This is how it will be with anyone who stores up things for himself but is not rich toward God.

Jesus Christ is the superlative example that has been set for us to follow. Jesus, the Light of this world is here for you. The Light of this world can be within you. As such, you have the power to change the world. Truly accept Jesus Christ as your personal Lord and Savior, and your life *will* change. Adapt to His teachings and you will achieve monumental blessings. Fortunately, to receive the gift of salvation from Jesus the Christ, there is no great mathematical formula to study and remember... There are no long theoretical models to learn.

To truly accept Christ, adapt to his teachings, and achieve richness toward God, simply follow two very short commandments:

1. *Love the Lord your God with all your heart and with all your soul and with all your mind; This is the first and greatest commandment.*

2. *And the second is like it: Love your neighbor as yourself.*

3. All the Law and the Prophets hang on... **two commandments.** (Mat 22:37-40)

Finally, as you face the Elevator of Life, always remember: it is not your heart that beats within; it is God's Heartbeat. *Act like it.* Lead your own life in a superlative fashion. Accept and adapt to His teachings, and you will achieve a higher plane of understanding. Adapt now; the time to change is *now!* Adapt as though your house is on fire, and the only way out is blocked. Adapt as if your life depends on it.

Your life *does* depend on it!

Achieve. After you truly accept God's will, and after you adapt to maximizing the good (selecting the "up" button), anything is achievable in the Hands of God. But you *will* continue to face adversity. When you do...

Consider this:
The way of a fool seems right to him...
But a wise man listens to advice. (Prv 12:15)

The advice of scientists and teachers revolves around proven concepts and historical teachings. In school, we learned about gravity and its great connective power throughout the vast universe. Somewhere along our path in life, we also learned about an all-powerful, omniscient, omnipotent God. However, much like the little bits of schooling we received throughout our lives, we seem to have forgotten so much of what we innately know about God. We seem to have somehow lost the knowledge that God does truly exist. And sadly, for some weird, strange reason, we continue to zip through our lives as if we own our first, last, and in-between heartbeats.

As one day is sewn into the next, it seems we put forth significant effort to keep our lives on a path that is pleasing to God. Yes, failure is a natural part of our imperfect human soul. And regardless of the ideology, man-made rules, laws, and ideas of this world will always fail. But God's grace is unfailing; no matter what good or bad acts you have done, life is still incomplete until you truly accept the will of God. Life *evolved from* God; our lives should *revolve around* God. Thus, *putting it all together* includes not only the act of incorporating God in your life, but also the **continuous** act of placing God's advice above everything else. Are you ready to "listen"?

15: Your Instructions from God

Knowledge is power. Wisdom is applied knowledge.
Thus, living a wise life is truly powerful.

~ John Clark

Parents of teenagers often lament about the tremendous trials and tribulations teenage children bring into their lives. I have heard many parents remark, *"Children don't come with an instruction book."* Moreover, some people claim that life itself does not come with an instruction book. Aside from the teachings of parents, some people believe life is best figured out by stumbling along until we get it right.

When my seventeen-year-old step daughter received her acceptance letter from the University of Michigan, my wife and I felt a mixed blessing of emotions. We were elated that she had achieved significant academic success. Yet, considering her naïve nature, procrastinating tendencies, and obvious lack of maturity, we were as worried about her future successes as we were proud of her previous accomplishments.

And when her freshman year ended with less-than-stellar grades and a strong warning from the university staff, our youthful protégé needed some seriously strong engagement from my wife and me.

But what can a parent do to *truly* influence the life of a teenager who has a new-found freedom in life? What can anyone do to influence other people? Indeed, portions of this very book advise you to simply accept the reality of your situation. And with regard to other people's actions, you simply cannot control people. The most you can ever hope to do is to accept who they are and try to influence the behaviors they exhibit.

In the United States, social behavior is constantly changing. But, for the most part, we are a country and society of laws. Those agreed-upon laws exist to influence our behavior. However, societal conduct itself is actually an influential input into the behaviors we consider appropriate or inappropriate.

In other words, if enough people agree to accept certain (inappropriate) behaviors, those same, previously unacceptable behaviors become acceptable... legally, morally, and ethically. Behavior previously considered inappropriate may ultimately be codified into legal proclamations from the various levels of the legislative and judicial branches of our multi-layered system of government. The associated legal repercussions (or punishments) are then proclaimed in the context of time served in jail or prison.

Regardless of how we feel about our current system of government, we are a civilized society as a result of the larger societal norms and values that have been constructed to ensure conformance to established rules, regulations, and laws.

Thus, we are all *influenced* by agreed-upon commandments. Many of these legalistic commandments are thrust onto society by a vast network of societal norms. Communities all across this great nation continue to pass ordinances, decrees, regulations, and a plethora of other legal rulings which must be followed by the inhabitants of the community.

From the homeowner association fee to the stop sign to the income tax, there are pages and pages of agreements by which we live. In theory, our nation's communities are a better, more civilized group of people because of these codified legal agreements.

However, the evening news is still fraught with reports of criminal behavior. Corporate boardrooms still fight corruption from within; violent criminals are still sentenced every day the courthouse is open; and shoplifting still accounts for a major portion of financial losses in retail establishments.

Are there laws against such behavior? Yes! But those laws cannot control society's behavior; those laws can only *influence* society's behavior.

What, then, can we do to influence others? More importantly, what can we do to influence our *self*?

When legal commandments continue to fail to successfully influence our youth, our spouses, and our corporate and political leaders, to what other commandments can we turn? To what other decrees should we turn? To what other instruction will *you* turn?

YOUR INSTRUCTION BOOK FOR LIFE

The Book of Proverbs is the answer. The *Book of Proverbs* is the instruction book for your life. If and when you follow the advice and instructions therein, you will **always** be on the right path; you will **always** choose the correct course; and you will **never** wonder, wander, or worry. You won't wonder if your path is leading in the right direction. You won't wander into the realm of the unprotected. And you will never have to worry about figuring out the complexities of life. Proverbial living is God's Plan for you.

Please note that the words *always* and *never* are literary superlatives. Authors must be very, very careful when using these particular words. And you, the reader of the author's work, must be very careful when considering advice from an author using these superlatives.

The *Book of Proverbs* is written specifically to give you superlative instruction on how to obtain wisdom and understanding about life. The *Book of Proverbs* is a manifestation of the two decrees of Jesus Christ:

Love the Lord thy God with all thy mind, body, and soul;
and Love thy neighbor as you love yourself.
(Mat 22:37-40)

The entire purpose of the *Book of Proverbs* can be summed up in the first few verses of the Book. The initial verses of the *Book of Proverbs* open with a very simple statement: The fear of the Lord is the beginning of knowledge. (Prv 1:7)   This one simple concept is overwhelmingly powerful, yet intricately simple. To fear the Lord God is a choice. It is also a beginning; not an end. Thus, choosing to fear God is a simple choice that you must make as an individual. No one can make this choice for you. Like the laws governing your speed on the highway, or your conduct when you are angry, or your responsibility to pay taxes on earned income, the books of the Bible are here to *influence* your behavior.

The *Book of Proverbs* admonishes you to fear the Lord God. And, like the commensurate monetary and jail-related repercussions associated with unacceptable behavior in society, there are corresponding penalties associated with choosing a life that lacks an honest, active fear of God. According to the *Book of Proverbs*, there is only one alternative to living a life with a fear of God; that alternative is a life as a fool. (Prv 1:7)

Thus, the choice is abundantly clear:
Choose knowledge or choose being a fool.

167

Undoubtedly, these are strong, forceful words. Many people may be taken aback by such a seemingly rigid sentiment toward those who choose not to believe in the words of the Bible. However, keep the following five logically connected points at the forefront of your mind:

1. Knowledge is power; wisdom is *applied* knowledge.
2. Thus, without knowledge, there can be no wisdom.
3. The fear of the Lord is the beginning of knowledge.
4. To deny God's existence is to deny knowledge.
5. Your choice is simple: choose to fear God; or be a fool.

By choosing God, you are choosing the Way of the Creator. By choosing God, you are selecting the way of the wise man. Accordingly, the following chapters deal directly with God's very specific instructions for you.

Chapters Sixteen through Eighteen provide a contemporary explanation of the concept of the *Book of Proverbs*. Chapters Nineteen through Twenty-Seven provide a brief synopsis of the first nine chapters of the *Book of Proverbs*. As you progress through the final few chapters of *God's Heartbeat*, remember the fundamental precepts of the earlier chapters: **life is painfully simple.**

How simple is life?

Well… we are born; we live; and we die. And in between our birth and death, we are to glorify God in all that we do. And it is just that simple. But first, we must accept God's presentation as the superlative perspective.

16: Proverbial Living: A Primer

The purpose of the *Book of Proverbs* is to help you attain wisdom and to be able to see Truth by adopting God's point of view as your own point of view. As I discussed earlier, perceptions are not really reality. Perceptions are based on a multitude of influential events, people, places, and self-sustaining beliefs that have slowly, surely, and strongly integrated their way into the manifestation that is you. Change your perception, and you will change you.

Your perceptions vary greatly in their relative comparison to the actual Truth and reality. Some of your beliefs are amazingly accurate. On the other hand, many of your preconceived notions are *incredibly **inaccurate***. But how do you know which perceptions are accurate and which notions are woefully incorrect? More importantly, what can you do to begin the process of changing and correcting your erroneous views while holding onto and strengthening the truthful aspects of your perceptions?

Fear not; the answer is painfully simple: throw everything away and start with Chapter One of the *Book of Proverbs*. You simply cannot go wrong with this God-given approach to life.

Have you ever baked a cake using a new recipe, cooked a meal using unfamiliar instructions, or lived a life without superlative guidance? Of course you have! If the cake comes out ruined and you don't quite know why; or if the meal ends  up completely unacceptable, you wouldn't try to sift through the acceptable and unacceptable parts of the food... and then try the exact same recipe a second time, would you?

First of all, you would not necessarily know how or why the overall creation turned out the way it did. Secondly, if you already have access to a different, proven recipe, why would you continue to use the new, unfamiliar, and historically bad recipe?

Likewise, the same concept applies in the creation of your new life. The *Book of Proverbs* presents a recipe for your new life. If you follow its simple instructions, the *Book of Proverbs* will guide you to be a wonderfully educated, wise, just, and equitable final product of a person. (Prv 1:3)

The instructions are simple. For example, you are advised to refuse the enticement of sinners because their feet lead to evil, and, in reality, they set up their own lives for failure. (Prv 1:10, 16, 18) Take a few moments and look back over the course of your life. Try to recall the influential nature of certain people in your life.

Some people had your best interests in mind; other people simply wanted you to join their evil crusade. Likewise, take time to look *forward* and do the same.

And life really is just that simple.

Please do not try to complicate this concept. People are who they are; your perception of their aptitude and charm has absolutely nothing to do with who they are at the core of their very being. Thus, be keenly aware when you are enticed to do things you *know* are wrong. To diminish the importance of this simple advice is pure foolishness.

At the same time, wherever there is an offer of treacherous behavior, there is *always* an alternate opportunity to refute or (if you insist on going forth with the behavior) to learn from the experience; to acquire a life of wisdom. (Prv 1:20) In other words, when you make the wrong choices in life (and we have all made some pretty bad choices at one time or another), **if** and **when** you learn from the experience, you will gain an insight and intelligence that can only be gained from those specific experiences. (Prv 1:23)

The learned incorporation of insight, intelligence, and experience, when fully integrated, is the true application of knowledge. The true *application of knowledge* is wisdom. But if you do not learn from your erroneous ways, you will, in effect, dumb yourself down. When you consistently choose the path of the unrighteous, you are actively choosing the path that is contrary to God's direction.

I will restate this concept again: every single day, you face choices that will take you in one of two vastly different directions. Those two directions include **God's path** or **another path**.

And life really is just that simple.

When you choose God's path, you are choosing knowledge. When you choose the alternate paths, you are choosing the opposite of knowledge; you are choosing ignorance. More importantly, you are choosing a life that is, quite literally, opposed to God (and opposed *by* God).

The *Book of Proverbs* has a very clear warning regarding the act of choosing alternate paths. If you don't choose God's path, you are refusing knowledge. If you are refusing knowledge, you will **never** attain wisdom. In fact, wisdom itself will elude you. (Prv 1:25-28) Specifically, "Then shall they call upon me [wisdom], but I will not answer; they shall seek me early, but they shall not find me: for that they hated knowledge and did not choose the fear of the Lord." (Prv 1:28, 29)

A few paragraphs back, when discussing the ruined cake, I mentioned that you would not necessarily know how or why the overall creation turned out the way it did. I also asserted that, if you have access to a different, proven recipe, why would you stick with the new or unfamiliar formula?

Here is another reason for starting a **new recipe for life**:

Jesus Christ says,
"What good will it be for a man if he gains the whole
world, yet forfeits his soul?

What can you give in exchange for your soul?"
(Matthew 16:26)

Seek not to save old bits and pieces from your former life.
Begin anew in a life as instructed by
the Living Word of God.

Begin a new life according to The Book of Proverbs.

17: Proverbial Living: The Academics

While earning my undergraduate degree, I learned that communication is comprised of four basic items: a sender; a message; a medium; and a receiver. At any given time, each of these four mutually exclusive items is equally important. In the context of *An Instruction Book for Your Life*, three of the four spiritual communication components are presented to you in the *Book of Proverbs*. The Sender (God), the Message (God's Word), and the Medium (The Holy Bible) comprise three of the four components of successful communication.

The sender, the message, and the medium
are all perfectly presented in
The *Book of Proverbs*.

The fourth component, the receiver is
You.

All the hard work has already been completed for you. All you have to do is take on the critically important role of the receiver. With or without you, the Sender remains the Alpha and the Omega. With or without you, the message remains equally eloquent.

However, without you, the medium (the Holy Bible) will collect dust as any other book on a shelf. And without the Sender's message being received by you, the world is a very empty place. But life should not have to be empty! *With you,* the Sender's message comes alive!

You can change the emptiness today, right here, right now. If you will simply choose to receive the words of guidance reflected in the medium of the Proverbs; if you endeavor to keep the two great commandments of Christ in your heart; if you simply use the Holy Bible as a way of asking God for understanding, you will eventually understand what it means to truly fear the Lord. And once you gain a basic understanding of the fear of the Lord, God will begin to give you knowledge, understanding, and wisdom. (Prv 2:1-6)

Ask yourself, "What does it mean to truly fear the Lord?" Do you have any idea who God is? Do you have the slightest inkling what God can do? Do you really and truly, absolutely, and unequivocally understand the fear of the Lord? Take a moment and ask yourself if you really, truly believe in the concept of an all-powerful, all-knowing, all-encompassing God of all creation.

Who is God to you? *What* is God to you?

Try this:

Take a few minutes; close your eyes.
And think about who and what God is.
Then open your eyes and see God again.

Once you begin to understand God, you will begin to clearly see the correct paths of righteousness. (Prv 2:9) Moreover, once you are on the right path, the Wisdom of God will actually work to keep you on the paths of righteousness and away from the paths of unrighteousness. (Prv 2:12) This Godly Wisdom is important because, in the course of living a Proverbial Life, you will be relentlessly challenged; you will be constantly attacked by people who simply delight in doing evil acts. (Prv 2:14) You must accept this coordinated, conspiratorial attack as a reality. Once you *accept* the reality of the veracity of evil-doers, you can *adapt* to their behavior by seeking further guidance from the Word of God. If and when you *accept* the evil-doers behavior and subsequently *adapt* by putting on the full armor of God by reading the Bible, you will *achieve* victory over your enemies. More importantly, you will *achieve an absolute victory over yourself.* And remember: Jesus said, "For whoever wishes to save his life will lose it; but whoever loses his life for My sake will find it." (Mat 16:26)

But first, you must play an integral role in the communication process. Today, as you read these words, the Sender, the Message, and the Medium all await the one act that only you can control.

Read on…

18: Proverbial Living: The Process

"We hold these truths to be self-evident, that all men are created equal, that they are endowed by their Creator with certain unalienable rights; that among these are Life, Liberty and the pursuit of Happiness" (United States Declaration of Independence, 1776).

Despite the wonderfully expressive imagery associated with the words of our great *Declaration of Independence*, the rights to life, liberty, and the pursuit of happiness are not guaranteed to or by anyone. Throughout the history of the United States, people were killed for "reasons" related solely to the amount of pigmentation in their skin (*no guarantee of life*). People were enslaved to ensure great commercial wealth to the status quo (*no guarantee of liberty*). And people were simply whipped (mentally, physically, and socially) into a vast, dark underclass that was systemically stripped of any hope for a better life (*no guarantee of a **viable** pursuit of happiness*). Thus, inasmuch as our founding fathers eloquently penned such lofty words, they also proved that the law of man is still subject to interpretation and application by men.

The Word of God is the Truest Law, the Highest Law.

THE SUPERLATIVE LAW

The *Book of Proverbs* advises you to never forget God's law and to keep God's commandments in your heart. (Prv 3:1) Your heart is where your life begins. Your heart is where your very life blood ebbs and flows; emits and returns. Your heart sets the *pace* for your blood and your life. You are advised to keep God's commandments in your inner core. Regularly scheduled physical exercise will keep your human heart healthy. Likewise, when you consistently seek and follow the teachings of God, your heart's content will be to seek additional teachings from God. As you seek greater Biblical Knowledge, you will grow in spiritual strength.

As you grow in spiritual strength and endurance, your life will begin to take on a certain spiritual glow. Believe me… the peacefulness associated with your life will grow in ways which you never thought possible!

However, you must *completely surrender* to the Word of God; you must trust in God while refraining from the desire to put God's Law in your mind (and not in your heart). For this reason you are admonished to "lean not to your own understanding." (Prv 3:5) In everyday life, you must acknowledge God. When you acknowledge God in everything that you do, He will direct your path. (Prv 3:6)

Don't wait until Sunday morning!

THE POWER OF PRAYER

But how do you acquire the discipline to *listen* to God? Where do you find the fortitude to repress your thoughts, interpretations, and applications on what is right? How do you gain the strength to stand up to family, friends, and "facts" that speak so negatively about the One True God? The answer is simple: you pray.

*Praying is essentially making a concerted effort to **pay attention** to the God who created this vast universe.*

To what should you pay the greatest attention?
To Whom should you pray the greatest attention?

Praying is telling God you need his assistance. Praying is submitting to the Will of God. Praying is accepting the relationship among and between you and God the Father. You are the servant; and there is a *supernatural* connection therein. Praying is adapting to the knowledge and applying the wisdom that God does, indeed, run things around here. Praying is achieving oneness with the One. Praying is your answer.

Do you want the discipline to listen to God? *Pray.* Do you want the fortitude to repress your thoughts, interpretations, and applications on what is right? *Pray.*

Do you want to acquire the strength to stand up to family, friends, and "facts" that speak so negatively about the One True God? *Pray.*

Do you want knowledge, wisdom, and a personal relationship with God? Pray. Do you want evil to prevail; do you want to follow your own understanding; do you want to live a life that is not recommended by God?

Then don't pray.

The choice is yours, only yours, and no one else's.

By totally trusting in a path directed by God, you will minimize the likelihood of wrecking your life with the "wise" decisions you *think* you are making. Thus, in all your ways, trust in the Lord with all of your heart.

HONOR GOD

I am constantly amazed when people try to define and confine God. The next time you find yourself trying to define God, or the next time you find yourself in a discussion with someone who wants proof of God, please remind them:

"God, the Creator...
> *... cannot be completely described by man,*
>> *...the created."*

This one, central point is critical to increasing your current level of faith. Man uses logic to seduce, deduce, and produce a multitude of people, ideas, and products, respectively. Man cannot use the basic premise of logic to seduce true Christians into disbelieving in the power of Jesus Christ. Man cannot apply the same earthly, rudimentary, man-made concept of logic to deduce a concept of the One True God.

"The wrath of God is being revealed from heaven against all the godlessness and wickedness of men who suppress the truth by their wickedness, since what may be known about God is plain to them, because God has made it plain to them.

For since the creation of the world God's invisible qualities—his eternal power and divine nature—have been clearly seen, being understood from what has been made, so that men are without excuse.

For although they knew God, they neither glorified him as God nor gave thanks to him, but their thinking became futile and their foolish hearts were darkened.

*Although they claimed to be wise, they
became fools and exchanged the glory of
the immortal God for images made to look
like mortal man and birds and animals and
reptiles.* " (Rom 1:18-23)

Man will *never* be able to produce anything remotely
resembling the might, majesty, and magnificence of the
One True God. Know it, love it, live it.

Accordingly, Proverbs advises you to honor the
Lord by giving the first fruits of your labor; you should do
it. Give freely and abundantly, and your personal
accounts will richly grow in return. (Prv 3:9-10) Again,
do not try to understand how this works. Lean not unto
your own personal understanding.

*As the heavens are higher than the earth,
so are my ways higher than your ways and
my thoughts than your thoughts.*
(Isaiah 55:9)

Simply follow the written word as it is written.
Follow the instructions in *The Instruction Book for Your
Life* and seek the wisdom therein. Indeed, you will
undoubtedly disagree with many admonishments along
the paths directed by God. However, just as a father
corrects his children out of love and a true desire to see
them succeed, God chastises His flock for their slight
deviations from His directed path. (Prv 3:11-12)

ARE YOU READY?

If you continue to seek God via knowledge and wisdom, you will find joy. Remember: *wisdom is applied knowledge*. By applying the knowledge gained through the Word of God, you will grow in your knowledge. As you grow and use your knowledge, you will become wiser. And as you continue to seek and apply the Teachings of God, you will attain an even higher plane of wisdom. When you reach the higher plane(s) of wisdom, you will be inspired to seek additional knowledge. When you acquire the newfound knowledge, you will have gained an entirely new set of skills, insights, and inspirations... each being (and bringing) an additional gift from the gracious God you serve.

Those new skills will allow you to solve greater problems. Those additional insights will allow you to see where you once were blind. Those newfound inspirations will cause you to cross canyons that you thought were too deep, too wide, or simply too hard. These new gifts from God are worth more than any number or type of jewels. (Prv 3:15) These new gifts will take you places your old self could never have imagined. These new gifts would never have been received if you had depended on your own earthly, logical understanding.

Understand this: The fear of the Lord is the beginning of knowledge. Listening to God is the acquisition of knowledge.

Only God Himself knows how the heavens were formed; only He knows how the oceans were initially created and how the clouds came to be.

Following the Lord's commandment is the truest application of knowledge; following the Lord's commandment is the first step on the path to wisdom.

By reading Proverbs, you can keep God's wisdom and direction in the forefront of your thoughts and close to your heart. (Prv 3:21) Moreover, you can be confident that your life decisions are in line with God's direction. (Prv 3:23) When you feel challenged by tumultuous events or turbulent times, you can feel safe and secure that the Will of God will work in your favor. (Prv 3:25)

Perhaps you feel a bit overwhelmed by the mere mention of the phrase *"evil-doers."* After all, we are in the twenty-first century, right? All the ghosts and goblins are long gone, right? Well, ask yourself if you believe in the Word of God. Research your personal theory on what makes a person good or bad. Ask yourself if you believe "our struggle is not against flesh and blood, but against the rulers, against the authorities, against the powers of this dark world and against the spiritual forces of evil in the heavenly realms." (Eph 6:12)

Ask yourself, "Am I ready to acknowledge that my heart beats because of God?" If you are ready, announce to the world today that yours is truly...

God's Heartbeat.

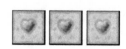

19: Proverbial Knowledge, Part I

God's knowledge awaits your decisive mind.

Chapter One of the *Book of Proverbs* is a simple, straightforward explanation of the **purpose** of the teachings. As the chapter states, The Proverbs are from Solomon, son of David, the former King of Israel. And the Proverbs exist to give the instruction of wisdom. As you progress through the last few pages of *God's Heartbeat*, perhaps you can place a Bible alongside this book and truly change your perspective; truly see the Proverbial Teachings come to life... *your* life.

Fear
The fear of the Lord is the beginning of knowledge: but fools despise wisdom and instruction. God is the only deity, and He should be respected as such. Your life is a gift from God; and you must thank Him with servitude, search, and sacrifice. This singular verse is the crux of God's Heartbeat. As stated earlier in the book, God has breathed life into you... Thus you are already inspired by God. However, you must now shift your perspective from an earthly view... to a view that is commensurate with a view more closely aligned with God's point of view. How do you do this? Serve God by seeking God and sacrificing the desires of the flesh. (Prv 1:7)

Listen

Hear the instruction of your Father. To receive the Word, you must quiet and separate yourself from the divisive noise of the world around you. Seek and serve him daily, hourly... and many times in between. Indeed, at various times, you must sacrifice your choice of entertainment, education, and fleshly edification. (Prv 1:8)

Learn

Do not waste your mind on the drivel of smutty television. Do not learn (or educate yourself to) the ways of the devilish world. Strengthen and edify your mind with the voice of God (the written Word of the Holy Bible). The general purpose of the *Book of Proverbs* is "to give subtlety to the simple, to the young man knowledge and discretion." (Prv 1:4) And, compared to God, we are all simple. Thus, we can all learn from Him. Knowledge, as the saying goes, is power. However, the smartest guy in the world can be easily outwitted by the simplest child... if the smartest guy does not use his knowledge. Thus, applied knowledge, or wisdom, is the true key to life. And regardless of what we face in life, or where we find ourselves, wisdom can be found waiting. Wisdom cries aloud; she utters her voice in the streets; she speaks at the mall, in the openings of the gates: in the city she utters her words, asking, "How long will you choose to hate knowledge?" (Prv 1:20-22)

Choose

Despite all the available books on health and wealth, there will always be death and poverty. Cigarette packaging is decorated with a very strong warning regarding the links between cancer and smoking; yet millions of people still smoke. Likewise, there will always be those that hate knowledge, and will not fear the Lord. Though our very own lives reflect the existence of a Higher Power, many people refuse to believe in God. There are also many people who profess a belief in God, yet choose to ignore His teachings. (Prv 1:29)

Reap

Your life will reflect the sum total of all your decisions. You will reap what you sow; you will eat of the fruit of your past. And, as such, you will suffer or be blessed from your own past plans. But if you seek Wisdom, you "shall dwell safely, and shall be quiet from fear of evil." But how do you "**seek wisdom**"? (Prv 1:31-33)

20: Proverbial Knowledge, Part II

A protected path awaits your chosen steps.

Chapter Two of the *Book of Proverbs* helps you to more fully appreciate the consequences of your actions... the good, the bad, and the ugly. The first few verses speak of your life's opportunities and possibilities; hence the word *"if"* used in verses 1-5. The latter verses detail the blessings you will receive "if" you keep the Father's commandments within your soul. These blessings are the positive consequences of your continuous walk in the Spirit of God. However, as the last few verses reflect, there are also those negative consequences that are sure to result when you forget your promises to God.

Choose
To seek wisdom, you must first actively and consciously choose to receive the Word of God. This is the fundamental choice of which I wrote in Chapter 13, *"Choose Your Superlative."* Once you choose a life that seeks to serve God, you must then choose to keep God's commandments. Keep them with you daily, hourly, *not* momentarily; you will soon find yourself seeking additional wisdom while simultaneously applying all that you have already learned. (Prv 2:1, 2)

Seek

When you earnestly seek the knowledge of God, and when you pray for understanding, you must humbly listen for His answers. If you treat and seek His knowledge as a superlative treasure, worth more than the finest of jewels... you will find a just reward.

Find

You will soon begin to understand what it means to fear the Lord. Indeed, if you diligently seek His knowledge, you will surely find the sought-after reward. This is a definitive statement of the Word of God. (Prv 2:3-5)

Receive

Once you find the true knowledge of God, you will gain a certain *synergistic* education. You will begin to see the world from an entirely different standpoint. You will soon see that all knowledge and understanding comes from God, and leads directly to wisdom. As you become interested in Truth and the teachings of God, you will be rewarded with a righteous lifestyle, greater knowledge, and increased wisdom. (Prv 2:6, 7)

Walk

Your increased wisdom will guide your path along God-given, protected paths. Your protected paths of heightened awareness will lead you to a greater appreciation for righteousness. Self-righteousness will no longer rule your life. Excuses and lies may have worked in earthly relationships... They won't work with God.

In a supernatural rite of educational passage, you will begin to see an enlightened path. Decisions will actually become easier to make. Your increased understanding will allow a greater sense of discretion as you face an evil world. Indeed, you will be delivered from evil and may not actually have knowledge of the deliverance... all because of the path God has illuminated and guided for you. But do not stray from the light into the dark; this is always your choice to make, wherever you are on your life's path. (Prv 2:8-13)

Keep
Stay focused on God; keep to His prescribed path. You will remain in His protected area. You are now armed with the knowledge from God; apply your knowledge and use it as a map to refrain from evil and remain in the land of the wise. (Prv 2:20-22)

21: Proverbial Knowledge, Part III

Truth and mercy will be made manifest in you.

Chapter Three of the *Book of Proverbs* speaks directly to and specifically of the expectations of a True Believer of God. Like the mother's child and the father's son, you should invest 100% of you and your trust in God.

This is not just an expectation. It is a directive; an edict; a decree. You *must* do this. This declaration is not a choice; it is something for which a child of God is **made**. Your heart beats because of God; it should now beat **for** God. If you are a child of God, do not try to decipher everything there is to know about life; do not lean to your own earthly understanding, but rather trust in Him with all of your heart.

Chapter Three is God's way of escorting you up to your spiritual hilltop and showing you the vast richness of Wisdom. Furthermore, He is telling you *how* to remain on that hilltop… how to remain close to Him.

As soon as you begin to honestly, truthfully, and prayerfully integrate His teachings into your life, your actions will begin to gain a certain momentum *toward* greater teachings, increased knowledge, and a better life. Your very own future path will become clearer to you… without much effort required on your part. Just as easily said as done!

Remember
To love God, never forget his commandments. (Prv 3:1)

Learn

Before you can remember (or forget) His commandments, you must learn how to fix your life upon the Word of God. (Prv 3:2)

Forgive

Ensure you forgive... just as Jesus forgives you for your transgressions. Seek Truth as much as you seek to forgive; for Truth and mercy are appreciated by both man and God. (Prv 3:3, 4)

Prioritize

Despite a tendency to rely on your own understanding, trust in God. Acknowledge Him in everything you do; everywhere you go; and with anyone who will listen. When you consistently acknowledge God, he will consistently guide your path. To walk a path illuminated by God is to be safe. All forms of evil are rendered powerless, and your allotted wealth will certainly increase when you put God first. (Prv 3:5-12)

Accept

Jesus was the only perfect "man" to walk the earth. As you walk along God's path, you will stumble. However, like the earthly father/son or father/daughter relationships, God will help correct your chosen path; don't be dismayed, but rather gladly accept His corrective teachings.

After diligently seeking God's wisdom, you will definitely find it. Thereafter, you will gain significant understanding, as well as a certain measure of happiness and honor, both of which are worth more than the finest jewels. True Wisdom is a cornerstone of the earth; and God has incorporated true Wisdom into the very nature of the earth. Thus, when you find true Wisdom, you are in alignment with nature. (Prv 3:12-20)

Lead
Place sound wisdom and spiritual discretion squarely at your front, and let them guide your steps. Do not underestimate their profound, positive effect on your life. (Prv 3:21, 22)

Follow
Do not be afraid of *anything*. Evil will surely make itself known to you. However, follow God, and you can rest easy. (Prv 3:23, 24)

Acknowledge
Give credit where it is due, and do it now. Be graceful in every way; love your neighbor and envy no one. Such is the life of the wise... those who shall inherit the glory of God. (Prv 3:27-35)

22: Proverbial Knowledge, Part IV

Learn and increase your level of Godly knowledge.

Chapter Four of the *Book of Proverbs* continues with a comparison and contrasting of the consequences resulting from your specific choices among the available options in life.

Indeed, God has given you the wonderful power of choice. You have your own free will. Quite a few pages of *God's Heartbeat* are dedicated to helping you to vividly see all the things to which you are paying attention. Please make this important: reconsider exactly how much *un-God-ly* information you are taking into your sponge-like mind.

Television shows and magazine articles are really one-way conversations, *during which you remain totally silent... taking it all in.* Verse 23 is especially relevant to the attention people tend to give to media. When you pay attention to so many different points of views, you are essentially being courted by many different choices. Why pay attention to so many different choices of amoral, asinine, apocalyptic nonsense... when you can choose the best teachings from God Himself?

Chapter Four of the *Book of Proverbs* is reminding you to accept the instruction of God; to keep that instruction; and to adapt your style of living to His knowledge-filled teachings.

Listen

Just as humble children listen to their caring fathers, take time to listen to your spirit; read the teachings of Christ, and align your life with the good doctrine He teaches. Pay attention to the very simple instructions. (Prv 4:1, 2)

Enjoy

Bathe in the attention of God. Like the only son of a dedicated father and mother, you are the center of God's attention. How much love does a mother have for her only son? How much teaching can one son receive from his father? Likewise, enjoy the focused love of an all-powerful God. (Prv 4:3)

Remember

As you grow in strength and determination, you will become more confident in your own newly acquired knowledge. Nonetheless, it is imperative to keep God's initial life lessons. Keep God's commandments. They are the foundations of life. More specifically, they are the foundations for *your* life. (Prv 4:4)

Grow

Continue to seek knowledge; then apply your learned knowledge. As your life is transformed by the resultant Wisdom, maintain a newer life that reflects the integration of your newfound knowledge, as well as the teachings you first received; *this* is Wisdom. You control your own actions. In fact, you can do almost anything you want.

Above all, though, **choose** to increase your own understanding, which is a precursor to knowledge and subsequent Wisdom. When you find knowledge, it will lead you to Wisdom. When you get Wisdom, you will face additional choices: keep learning, or forget and fail. Choose to exalt and embrace Wisdom, and you will increase your own knowledge, understanding, value in the eyes of God. Choose the Wisest path. (Prv 4:5-11)

Choose
Your life is filled with a continuous stream of choices. Once you choose to increase your own understanding, your path ahead becomes crisp, clear, and, most importantly, comprehensible to you. Indeed, you will begin to understand why things are the way they are. Moreover, because of the clarity of your path, you will begin to more easily see the correct connection from your current path to the upcoming fork in the road. Yes, when you choose Wisdom, you are choosing calm over calamity; clarity over confusion; and understanding over uncertainty. The choice is ultimately yours. (Prv 4:11-22)

Avoid
Stay focused on the Word of God; foremost in your mind. When you see evil, do not pretend you don't see it; turn from it, and protect your Godly life. Ensure you steer absolutely clear of evil; merely passing by the evils of this world will only risk your own Godly life. (Prv 4:22-27)

23: Proverbial Knowledge, Part V

Align your life accordingly.

Chapter Five of the *Book of Proverbs* begins a metaphorical comparison and discussion of the "strange woman." The strange woman represents more than the literal, physical aspects of an earthly woman. Indeed, men would certainly do well if they remain wary of strange, smooth-talking women.

However, there is a beautifully blended allegory, if not double entendre within Chapter Five. The allegory of the strange woman provides a very powerful warning to stay away from strange teachings that are antithetical to the teachings of God. This admonition is as relevant today as it was hundreds of years ago. You simply *must* be wary of all the traps, tricks, and treacherousness of evil. Never underestimate the power of evil.

At first glance, you may or may not agree with this particular assessment of Chapter Five. However, take some time and study the chapter, especially in context and relation to the other adjoining chapters. Notice that the other adjoining chapters all discuss the absolute purity and associated search for Wisdom. The allegorical shift in Chapter Five is meant to draw a physical and spiritual parallel among the wiles of the world, and the world of the wise.

Listen

To learn, you must first choose to listen. To grow in any manner, you must initially listen to God's message and subsequently build your logical and supernatural understanding upon His superlative knowledge. This is a very critical point of understanding: listening is not merely being quiet.

Think

Listening to God includes using your mind, body, and soul to incorporate additional knowledge into your own synapses (brainwork) and lifestyle. You are not a born talker; you *learned* how to speak. You were not a born mathematician; someone else *taught* you how to add and subtract. Likewise, God has much to teach you about the world in which you live. Listen and learn from your Best Teacher. (Prv 5:1, 2)

Beware

Be very wary of alternate teachings. Many alternative views of god(s) exist throughout the world. Yet, there is only One True God. Despite the notorious claims of people throughout history, it is important to remember that Jesus said, "I am the way and the truth and the life. No one comes to the Father except through me." (John 14:6) Indeed, when you seek knowledge, Wisdom, and Truth, begin your quest with the knowledge that God is the only constant in this world. He is the Alpha and Omega, the Beginning and the End. (Rev 22:13)

Avoid

Avoid other teachings that change like the latest fad. The way of God is the way of life; all other teachings are simply paths in direct conflict with the path of God. More to the point, they are paths to death. The Spirit of God represents the Highest Form of Knowledge; it very well *is* the Highest Form of Knowledge. Thus, when you choose to follow teachings that are not aligned with the Spirit of God, you deliberately pass your God-given blessings to other people who couldn't care less about you, your family, or your lasting legacy. (Prv 5:3-11)

Reflect

Dedicate significant personal time to look at your true self and compare yourself to the prescribed teachings of Christ. Do not become self-righteous, and do not shirk or hide from the guilty convictions you will undoubtedly face; your convictions reflect the perfect trajectory of a life preparing for change. (Prv 5:12-14)

Practice

Introspective reflection (looking inside at your true self) allows you to be honest with yourself. Be sure to practice what you preach. Lying to others may appear helpful, but, in reality, God sees and knows everything. (Prv 5:15-20)

24: Proverbial Knowledge, Part VI

Complete the covenant to serve God Almighty.

Chapter Six is all about preparation and separation. This chapter continues with cautionary allegories and examples from the physical world. As a child of God, you should diligently work to seek and find Wisdom. Remember: knowledge is applied Wisdom. First you must seek knowledge; and, once you find and possess knowledge, then you can find Wisdom.

But to obtain knowledge, you must start at the beginning... According to the first chapter in the *Book of Proverbs*, "fear of the Lord is the **beginning** of knowledge"... but that's just the beginning. From whom much is given, much is expected. So you must build upon your beginning; plan for your end.

And, as Chapter Six relates, there are very specific things that God overtly hates. This chapter delineates seven specific acts that you simply should not do.

There is no room for doubt, no space for discussion, and no time for explanations. Take a few moments in time and learn these seven items. Learn how to live a life that is full of God, and not full of these seven things: a proud look, a lying tongue; hands that shed innocent blood; hearts that devise wicked imaginations; actions that proactively seek evil deeds; lies; and actions seeking to stir up trouble and strife.

The allegorical comparisons continue with an example of the industrious ant... the ultimate preparer. Enthusiastically social insects, ants can lift things that weigh more than three times their own body weight... and they are constantly busy preparing for the next chapter in their tiny little lives.[12] What are you currently doing to prepare for the next chapter in your spiritual life? A second allegory involves using God's commandments as a lamp, brightly illuminating your path ahead in life. Finally, the chapter ends with another warning to stay away from the "tongue of the strange woman." And, again, this is a stern admonishment to keep to God's prescribed path and steer clear of the seductress world.

Refrain
At some point in your spiritual journey, you will consider yourself committed to a certain style of life; a specific lifestyle that is reflective of your Chosen Superlative, God the Creator. However, if you don't truly commit yourself to a Proverbial life, your words are mere promises, and those promises fall far short of action. Refrain from making empty commitments.

Focus
In this life, your actions are paramount; and only God knows your exact thoughts and your future next actions. Similarly, you can never know what someone else is thinking or planning. Thus, refrain from making agreements on behalf of others. Focus agreements on your specific actions and plans. (Prv 6:1-4)

Consider

By focusing on yourself, you can attain a higher level of personal leadership. Over the course of a lifetime, your life may not be *optimized* for praising God. In fact, many Christians tend to say other people make them mad. They may act as if they are not in control of their own destiny, and they blame others for their personal planning mistakes. Consider yourself the co-pilot of your life; God is the Pilot.

Emulate

Interestingly, the tiny ant, with no leader to follow, does exceedingly well. How does she achieve such consistent success? The prosperous, well-prepared ant plans for her future without being directed. Likewise, you will achieve personal success if, like the industrious ant, you take time to prepare now; prepare for the future harvest of souls. (Prv 6:6-8)

See

Truth is what is. However, sometimes we try to convince ourselves that our respective perception is the actual Truth. In reality, the (Capital 'T') Truth is the **only** Truth. In today's world, people readily accept little white lies, and invest time in a television genre called *reality TV*. There is no such thing as reality TV. There is only *your* reality. See it for what it is: *your* reality. Likewise, evil is evil, no matter how it is manifested. Learn to recognize it. (Prv 6:12-15)

Know

The best way to recognize evil is to *educate yourself* on the seven things that God specifically hates. God hates a proud look, a lying tongue, and hands that shed innocent blood. God hates a heart that devises wicked imaginations. God hates when people proactively seek evil deeds. God hates when people lie on one another. And God literally hates when people seek to stir up trouble. Know and avoid these seven specific abominations. (Prv 6:16-19)

Commit

As a committed Christian, you should seriously consider how you live your life. Christians acknowledge and honor God in all of their daily activities. Honor God by refusing to flirt with other lifestyles. (Prv 6:24-35)

25: Proverbial Knowledge, Part VII

Be filled with Wisdom, leaving room for nothing else.

Chapter Seven leaves no doubt about the allegorical admonitions related to the strange woman. In fact, this chapter serves to provide the strongest possible warning of the possible onslaught of evil headed your way. As stated earlier in *God's Heartbeat*, you should never underestimate the power of denial. Likewise, you should never underestimate the power of evil, or to what extent evil will go through to get its worldly grasps into your soul.

Chapter Seven relates the other-worldly teachings as a woman, dressed as a harlot, and shifty at heart. This is a direct reflection of the *beautifully ugly* offerings of the world. Yes... the beautifully ugly offerings of which you can partake with your own free will. And if you think your spiritual faith is impenetrable, consider Verse 13: She took hold of him and kissed him, and with a brazen face she said, "I have ... offerings at home." Later, Verses 26-27 say, "Many are the victims she has brought down; her slain are a mighty throng. Her house is a highway to the grave, leading down to the chambers of death."

Therefore please be forewarned. If you will simply listen... *truly* listen to and continuously seek Wisdom, you will successfully fend off the advances of teachings that are not perfectly aligned with God.

Remember

God is our Heavenly Father, we should *diligently* seek to understand, remember, and apply His commandments. The Author of *all* life, He is uniquely qualified to provide direction for your specific life and the path of your exact journey. (Prv 7:7:1)

Delight

Proverbs advises you to delight in Proverbial Law and treat it as "the apple of your eye." This is an interesting idiom that deserves more than a cursory comparison. Apples are often used as a symbol of good health or great fortune. Some people believe this idiom originates with a belief that the smaller, dark, center opening in the eye was a solid, spherical ball; thus, the small "apple in the eye" is also the core of our world.

Compare

It has been said the eyes are windows to the soul. Your eyes represent a gateway into your heart. Everything you see is ultimately planted firmly in the center of your mind. Shield your heart like dark glasses shading your physical view of the world. Moreover, as you receive (good or bad) information into your mind, that information becomes a part of you (like the words on this page, for example). But what will you *do* with this information after you have received it? As you continue to learn new ideas, gain new abilities, and meet new people, you must choose specific follow-on actions.

The benchmarks to which you compare your lifestyle, and the lens through which you view the world should be changed and based upon God's precepts... not television, supermodels, or superstars. (Prv 7:1, 2)

Remind

God's commandments are extremely important. But is God *really* that important to you? To fully understand, appreciate, and adapt to spiritual living, you should literally fixate on God's teachings throughout your day. "Bind [His teachings] upon thy fingers; write them upon the table of your heart." (Prv 7:3)

Seek

If you ever grow weary of your constant search for knowledge, reconsider the true value of God-given Wisdom. Consider the vast expanse of evil existing in this world, and realize that you are extremely vulnerable to the wicked forces of this world. Indeed, you are walking through the Valley of the Shadow of Death. Sometimes death is as sudden as a plane crash. But for the educated Christian, a slow spiritual death is far less noticeable, and equally final. By ceaselessly seeking God's Wisdom, you will fill your personal well with His teachings, leaving absolutely no room for the world's temptations. (Prv 7:4-27)

26: Proverbial Knowledge, Part VIII

Allow God's Wisdom to rule your living world.

Chapter Eight moves from the allegorical references of the earlier chapters... to an outright one-way discussion from Wisdom Herself. Again, please notice the gender references. Wisdom is represented as a woman whose ways are known and whose company reaps rich rewards.

She is an illuminator of paths, and a protector of princes, kings, and other rulers who learn to listen to her established ways. On the other hand, the afore-mentioned woman of ill-repute, the strange woman who entices mysteriously... only offers dark paths leading to certain death. The choice is certainly yours. But with such an easily contrasted life, why on earth would you consciously choose teachings contrary to the Wisdom of God? Chapter Eight finishes with a powerful insight into exactly *who* Wisdom is.

She was with God when He created heaven and earth. She was here and there when He parted the oceans. She is here now, awaiting your decision to choose Her. And if you are *still* not quite clear on the overt consequences associated with your opportunistic choices, take a gander at the final two verses of the chapter:

Whoever finds [Wisdom] finds life and receives favor...

But whoever fails to find [Wisdom] harms himself;

And all who hate [Wisdom] love death.

Stop!

Take a look at everything you have read and subsequently learned about life. Ponder your previous path and consider the challenging periods of your life. As you look back, the benefit of hindsight allows you to see if your previous decisions were, indeed, correct... or if your choices were less than perfect. In reality, all of your decisions are important. However, people rarely see or understand how their own personal wisdom is integrated into their decision-making process. At a red stoplight, drivers exercise great wisdom when yielding to oncoming traffic. In our spiritual life, Wisdom is always present, waiting for us to yield and listen. (Prv 8:1-5, 33)

Listen

A recurring theme within the *Book of Proverbs*, **listening** is the foundation for learning. Another key action is to learn by doing. Some well-seasoned grandparents know experience is a tough teacher; it will test you first, and leave the questions for later. When you seek God's Wisdom, you consent to listening to and learning from the Creative Source of man!

Do not complicate this simple Truth.

Once again, I ask: do you believe in God? If you believe in God, defer to His omniscient omnipotence. He knows you well; listen to Him. (Prv 8:6-11)

Value
When you envision the last years of your life, what images ease across your mind? Will you relax as a wealthy retiree? Or will you work until your body demands *final* relaxation? Answers to these questions depend on your current system of values. We all enjoy the finer things in life. However, Proverbs advises you to apply the greatest value to the acquisition of Wisdom; for this is an achievement in and of itself. (Prv 8:10-21)

Live
Take a personal inventory of your daily life. Who are your friends? What type of people do you most often associate? Do you walk along the straight path of life, or are you on a wide corridor leading to destruction? This is a very simple question, and the answer does not require much thought. Indeed, if you need time to think about your answer, perhaps you should consider narrowing your path. God prefers a life of prudence. (Prv 8:12)

Find
When God created the heavens and the earth, Wisdom was there. When He created the mountains, valleys, oceans, and fields... Wisdom was there. When you gain God's Wisdom, you gain insight into the very Creation of life, a special favor from the Lord. (Prv 8:22-36)

27: Proverbial Knowledge, Part IX

Choose your superlative. Everything else will follow.

Accept
Food and shelter are the basic necessities for life. Without a doubt, you will die without proper nutrition and adequate shelter. Of course, you can probably skip several meals and still survive through one or two snowstorms. However, if you have access to a big house, warm bed, and delicious meals, why would you choose to spend several hungry hours facing the harsh elements? Likewise, there is a festival of knowledge awaiting your arrival. A strong House of Wisdom has been built, and the table therein is full of delectable treats for you and your love ones to enjoy. Accept God's invitation to a profoundly insightful life. (Prv 9:1-3)

Adapt
At this point, you should be well aware of the significance of God's Wisdom. And whether or not you have previously seen it as such, Wisdom is the partner and very Foundation of the world. From here, you really only have one decision regarding two possible choices. From this point forward, you can establish yourself as a person who builds upon the Foundation of Proverbial knowledge and subsequently apply your newfound information in every walk of your life. If you choose to do this, you will have transformed your rudimentary understanding into a life of superior wisdom. (Prv 9:4-6)

On the other hand, you can simply continue to walk along the dark, uninformed path, littered with people who foolishly revile knowledge, thoughtlessly flail through life, and aimlessly wander directly into the jaws of evil and a subsequent spiritual or literal death. Avoid making the wrong decision. Adapt to a prudent lifestyle and start your new path with an Eternal Light from God. Keep this Lamp lit by exercising an hourly appreciation for God, and all that he is doing for you. Remember: like the only child of a doting mother and father, you are the recipient of a focused, altruistic, incomparable, supernatural love. Thank God for His Love.

Achieve

When you simply acknowledgment the existence of God, you are doing well. But remember; wickedness prevails on many levels (and evil itself is well educated on the power of God). Thus, to better understand and relate with God, you must attain a healthy, fearful respect for the One True God. Once you accept and truly believe in the existence of God, you will begin adapting your lifestyle to an existence that reflects you're the very reason your heart beats.

When you accept God and enthusiastically adapt to the Proverbial quest for knowledge, your spiritual path becomes abundantly clear; your life develops via Divine Intervention. Indeed, when you accept and adapt to God's Wisdom, you will achieve your heart's content.

Tonight, your heart's content is to be God's Heartbeat.

As discussed in the *"Acknowledgments"* (at the end of *God's Heartbeat*), the *Book of Proverbs* is philosophically structured into two distinctive parts. In *God's Heartbeat*, I have provided a focus on Chapters One through Nine, which speak directly to the absolute, unequivocal, and very real results that are achieved when you consistently seek knowledge and wisdom.

On the other hand, Chapters Ten through Thirty-one provide very detailed directions on how to handle specific situations in life. I encourage you and your family to actively research and discuss the wealth of information and observations available in The *Book of Proverbs*, Chapters Ten through Thirty-One. Each of the verses can be applied to a wide array of situations. I am confident you will find one that speaks to a topic near and dear to your heart.

28: It is Finished

Let's review.

Whether you want to talk about it now, deal with it later, or pretend like it's just not going to happen... sooner or later, you will face death. Like the choice that greets you as you face the elevator doors, your style of living is a choice. Your Elevator of Life is called by you, and it can open up a whole new world in and out of your mind. You live in a world where the key to life is acceptance. May I have your attention for a few more pages?

You've trusted me this far... why stop now?

Your personal change begins now; this minute.

Do not wait until your life account is closed or overdrawn. Though the average heart beats almost three billion heartbeats in a lifetime, can you guess when your heart will suddenly stop?[13] Think about it... are you above or below average? Will your heart beat a little more than average... or a few beats below? At this point in the book, and at this point in your life, I hope and pray that you have literally no interest in thinking about the "average person." However, if you still want to know a little something about the average man or woman, go visit them at their house on Main Street.

They live right down the street from the Easter Bunny and around the corner from Santa Claus...

Perhaps you think I'm trying to be cute or dismissive. Perhaps this book seems a bit cavalier about the phrase *"average people."* However, think about the synonyms for "average": middling; run-of-the-mill; typical; common.

Which of those adjectives would you choose to describe yourself? Which of those adjectives would you use to define and describe your relationship with God? Do you stand out as a very, very strong, knowledgeable Christian... well-read on the *Book of Proverbs* and the *Teachings of Christ*; or are you a middling, mild-mannered pew warmer? Do you want to be known as a follower of Christ; or are you a run-of-the-mill member of the church? Are you a basketball fan(atic); or are you a Jesus fan(atic)? The choice is yours, and yours alone.

ACCEPT ADAPT ACHIEVE

God's instructions are clear. In fact, His instructions are simple, straightforward, and superlative:

1. **Accept** Jesus Christ as your Lord and Savior;
2. **Adapt** to His teachings and learn to love the Lord God with all of your mind, heart, and soul.
3. **Achieve** a level of knowledge and understanding that is possible only when you change your presentations, propensities, and priorities...

But first, you must accept; then you can adapt; then you will achieve. You now **know** what it takes to permanently change your life. Take a look at the Table of Contents in this book; it is a roadmap to living a Christian life. Specifically, you already have your own personal story to live; but first you must decide if you believe an age-old question: is it one life or two? The Elevator of Life can certainly take you to a whole new world, but only if you accept the Key to life.

Please pay attention to the last words of this chapter.
You have already received your instructions from God.
When you fall asleep tonight, listen to your heartbeat.
When you wake again, say to yourself, "It is finished."

Those were the last words of Jesus Christ, just before His Spirit ascended into Heaven. In His death and resurrection, you have already been **given** a new life. Your old life is now finished.

Begin a new life for God.

Accept his Gift;
Adapt to His teachings;
Achieve a new life.

"It is finished"

Acknowledgments

In all your ways acknowledge him;
And he will make your paths straight. (Prv 3:6)

Far beyond the title of this book, and in every aspect of my being, I acknowledge God as the Creator of this work. Though portions of this book have evolved over many years of writing, thinking, and praying, God was always there. To be sure, I have not always listened to His voice, and I have certainly failed to apply all of His teachings all of the time. But He has **never** failed me. And this work is a testament to both my faith in Him, and His partnership with me.

Long ago, as cornerstones in the foundation and creation of my life and faith, my mother, father, and grandmothers set in motion a series of events that could not have been known when they schooled me on Sunday mornings, read to me stories from the Bible, or simply said grace with me at the table. I truly thank them for the birth, life, and education of John H. Clark, III; I will continue to honor them with my life, and always respect them with all of my heart and mind. Thank you Mom, Momma, and Pops.

For as long as I can remember, I have always valued true friendship. Though I have been acquainted with numerous people over the years, and despite my world travels, my circle of friends is relatively small. Some of my best friends are members of my family, including my cousin, Trina, and my mother, Anita. And though a simple friendship is an asset worthy of the highest regard, I have found altruistic camaraderie to be a rare experience. To those few who have helped me to help myself by allowing me to ponder with you over the years, I am eternally indebted. Mr. Joshua Tucker and Ms. Tamela Aikens have helped me in this regard. Thank you for our respective true, lifelong friendships.

To the Chief Petty Officer Community of the United States Navy, I am indebted in a way that may never be understood. As a prior-enlisted officer, I am educated in the technical aspects of the apprentice as well as the managerial facets of the leader. In 1986, at the age of eighteen, I enlisted in the United States Navy, intent on seeing the world outside of Michigan. After initial training in the Navy's Basic Electricity and Electronics School in San Diego, California, I was assigned to Data Systems Technician School, a more specialized computer school in Mare Island, California.

During the initial months at Mare Island, an unassuming Navy Chief Petty Officer reviewed my personnel file and suggested I apply for an officer accession program. The Navy Chief, whose name I wish I knew, initiated a chain of events that altered my naval career in a most profound manner. Because of his direct efforts, I was selected to attend a little-known program called Broadened Opportunity for Officer Selection and Training (BOOST), an intensive year-long college prep school specializing in Calculus I and II, Physics I and II, and English Literature, among other academic disciplines. Upon completion of BOOST, I was awarded a Naval Reserve Officer Training (NROTC) scholarship and a commission as an ensign in the United States Navy.

Undeniably, that Chief Petty Officer saw something unique and different in me and my personnel file. Most importantly, though, he *did* something about it; he invested his time, energy, and enthusiasm in me, a young man with whom he had neither a familial link nor a friendly connection. Thank you, Chief, wherever you are.

Regardless of your religious or philosophical past, I pray you can appreciate the altruistic nature of the *Book of Proverbs*. Moreover, I humbly acknowledge the rights and privilege of other people to profess a belief in their own respective God. And inasmuch as I profess a staunch belief in the resurrection of Jesus Christ, I ask every reader of these words to keep an open mind.

God's Heartbeat, as well as the *Book of Proverbs*, is a straightforward discussion on the path to knowledge, wisdom, and God. Keep in mind, the *Book of Proverbs* is a part of the *Old Testament* of the *Holy Bible*.

Accordingly, regardless of your professed faith, (*Christianity, Islam, Agnostic, Atheist, Hinduism, Chinese traditional religion, Buddhism, primal-indigenous, African Traditional & Diasporic, Sikhism, Juche, Spiritism, Judaism, Baha'I, Jainism, Shinto, Cao Dai, Zoroastrianism, Tenrikyo, Neo-Paganism, Unitarian-Universalism, Rastafarianism, Scientology, or any other*) , please know that, by reading the contents of the *Book of Proverbs*, no one is disparaged for walking their own path, selecting their own destination, or professing a different version of The Deity.

My only proclamation regarding *Proverbs* is that a life based on its teachings is virtually guaranteed to result in a spiritually enriched, joyous life; an acknowledgment of the powerful premise and life-altering principles espoused therein.

The *Book of Proverbs* is philosophically structured into two distinctive parts. In *God's Heartbeat*, I focus on the first part, Chapters One through Nine. The first nine chapters speak directly to the absolute, unequivocal, and very real results that can be achieved when you consistently seek knowledge and wisdom according to God's Teachings.

On the other hand, the remaining Chapters Ten through Thirty-one, provide very detailed directions on how to handle specific situations in life.

For example, Proverbs, 4:23 says, *"Above all else, guard your heart, for it is the wellspring of life."* This is a philosophical reference to being true to yourself, primarily because innermost desires, good or bad, will become reality.

Conversely, Proverbs 31:10 says, *"A wife of noble character who can find? She is worth far more than rubies."* This question and comparative answer is rhetorical, literal, and more than a philosophical description of a good wife.

Interestingly, the final verses and last words of the *Book of Proverbs* speak directly and plainly about the value of a good woman. Quite simply, the final words of *Proverbs* discuss the type of woman who has the potential to affect every single person on this planet.

A good woman is...

A great sister, a wonderful daughter, a special aunt, a talented niece, a calming cousin, and a sensational friend.
A good woman is, indeed, the grandest grandmother.
And, as I have lovingly learned, a good woman is

A great wife and...

A magnificent gift from God.

Thus, it is with great pleasure and love that I save my greatest acknowledgement for last. My wife, Delia, has been a Godsend as I have endeavored to publish *God's Heartbeat*. Though God is certainly the Editor-in-Chief, my wife, Delia has been a patient, persistent, and pretty senior editor. Much more than that, though, she has been the water to my well; she is the mortar to my brick; and she is the Love of my life.

And though I have a sincere respect for the power of words, mere words will never convey the absolute joy she has afforded me in the years we have shared. She is more than a companion; she is my spiritually connected crusader. She is my opposite, of which there can be no greater bond.

She is my good woman.

Notes

Page iv. "Joyce Cary: Definition and Much More from Answers.com," http://www.answers.com/topic/joyce-cary (Accessed July 30, 2008)

Page 59. Archbold, Rick, Robert Ballard, and Ken Marschall. *PBS Online - Lost Liners - Titanic.* http://www.pbs.org/lostliners/titanic.html (Accessed July 9, 2008).

Page 86. "Officials: U.S. submarine hit undersea mountain," http://www.cnn.com/2005/US/01/10/nuclear.submarine.update/index.html (Accessed July 9, 2008).

Page 93. Simon, Paul. "Bridge over Troubled Water." <u>Bridge over Troubled Water.</u> Columbia Records, 1968.

Page 93. "N C H S - FASTATS - Life Expectancy", http://www.cdc.gov/nchs/fastats/lifexpec.htm (Accessed July 9, 2008)

Page 95. "U.S. and World Population Clocks - POPClock. July 5, 2008." http://www.census.gov/main/www/popclock.html

Page 96. Darrell Ames, "Thresher-Scorpion disasters resulted in safer Submarine Navy." http://www.csp.navy.mil/centennial/589-593.htm (Accessed July 9, 2008)

Page 102. "Are Earthquakes Really on the Increase?" July 5, 2008. http://earthquake.usgs.gov/learning/topics/increase_in_earthquakes.php (Accessed July 9, 2008).

Page 102. "Safety and security for travelers, vehicles, and transportation systems", http://www.bts.gov/publications/transportation_statistics_annual_report/2006/html/chapter_01/safety_and_security.html (Accessed July 9, 2008)

Page 152. "The Solar System", (Accessed July 9, 2008). http://www.kidsastronomy.com/the_planets.htm

Page 156. "You deserve a break today", from the 1971 advertising campaign of McDonalds Corporation.

Page 208. "Ant, Ant Profile, Facts, Information, Photos, Pictures, Sounds, Habitats, Reports, News - National", http://animals.nationalgeographic.com/animals/printable/ant.html (Accessed July, 28, 2008)

Page 223. "Heart - MSN Encarta", http://encarta.msn.com/encyclopedia_761572608_3/Heart.html#p21 (Accessed July 9, 2008)

About the Author

John H. Clark III, a career Naval Officer, with an MBA from the Naval Postgraduate School, gained newfound freedom after an abbreviated deployment to Iraq. His journey of discovery led him to a profound Truth about life and God's instructions for us all. An author, poet, and mentor, he lives with his wife and daughters in Virginia.

PHOTO AND COVER ART COURTESY of BFG PRESS

For additional resources
visit the *God's Heartbeat* website:

www.Gods-Heartbeat.com

Printed in the United States
121990LV00002B/1-117/P